Called or Collared?

Other books by Francis Dewar

Give Yourself a Break
(Hunt & Thorpe 1992)

Invitations – God's calling for everyone
(SPCK 1996)

Live for a Change: discovering and using your gifts
(2nd edition, Darton, Longman & Todd 1999)

FRANCIS DEWAR

Called or Collared?

AN ALTERNATIVE APPROACH
TO VOCATION

SPCK

First published in Great Britain 1991
SPCK
Holy Trinity Church
Marylebone Road
London NW1 4DU

New edition 2000

Unless otherwise indicated, biblical quotations are from
The New Revised Standard Version of the Bible ©1989

British Library Cataloguing in Publication Data

A catalogue record for this book
is available from the British Library

ISBN 0–281–05350–2

Typeset by Deltatype Ltd, Birkenhead, Merseyside
Printed in Great Britain by
The Cromwell Press, Trowbridge, Wiltshire

Contents

I pray that, according to the riches of his glory, he may grant that you may be strengthened in your inner being with power through his Spirit, and that Christ may dwell in your hearts through faith, as you are being rooted and grounded in love. I pray that you may have the power to comprehend, with all the saints, what is the breadth and length and height and depth, and to know the love of Christ that surpasses knowledge, so that you may be filled with all the fullness of God.

Now to him who by the power at work within us is able to accomplish abundantly far more than all we can ask or imagine, to him be glory in the church and in Christ Jesus to all generations, forever and ever. Amen.

Ephesians 3.16–21

Preface

This is a book about the calling of God. Our notion of calling or vocation has become very narrowed, and is often taken only to mean the calling to be an ordained minister. Even when it includes other occupations and other spheres it often carries with it the connotation that it is a job, paid, full-time, life-long, and one that requires special professional qualifications. I want to rescue the idea from all those assumptions because I believe that God calls every human being, if only we can learn to listen. He calls us to himself and he calls each of us to some particular self-giving task at each stage of our life. The calling of God is as wide and as varied as that, and it is for everyone. I have already written about this in *Live for a Change* (Darton, Longman & Todd, 2nd edition, 1999), which offered the general reader a DIY approach to exploring the issue of God's calling in their own life and circumstances.

As a result of the success of that book Judith Longman of SPCK asked me to write a book from a similar standpoint but addressed particularly to would-be ordinands in the Church of England, since if there is any truth in this approach it clearly has implications for them and also for the serving clergy of the Church. I had already canvassed the basic ideas in an article in *Theology* in 1985. These were subsequently taken up in *Call to Order*, a report by the Advisory Board of Ministry of the Church of England in 1989 (known as ACCM at that time). So it was clear that they were of some interest to those entrusted by the Church with the selection and training of ordinands.

At first, I thought it would be a difficult but not impossible task. As I got down to it and began to feel a real enthusiasm and commitment to it, it was soon borne in upon me that it was in fact not possible. I do not think that at this point in the history of the

Church of England it is possible to write a book for would-be ordinands that will be helpful to all. The diversity of people in that position today is simply too wide.

So it is as an older and, I hope, slightly wiser person that I lay down my pen and offer these pages to such readers as will bear with me. It is in no sense the last word on the subject, but I very much hope it will be of use and even of real encouragement and enlightenment to many. I hope too that it will be read by people who have no interest in being ordained, but who want to be responsive to God's calling to them. They could with advantage skip the last chapter, and also the second half of chapter 1.

In the end, I take comfort from the worldly-wise author of Proverbs – 'a flood of words is never without its fault' (Prov. 10.19) – and encouragement from one of Anthony de Mello's quirky stories:

> Said a traveller to one of the bystanders, 'I have travelled a great distance to listen to the master, but I find his words quite ordinary.'
> 'Don't listen to his words. Listen to his message.'
> 'How does one do that?'
> 'Take hold of his sentences. Shake them well till all the words drop off. What is left will set your heart on fire . . . .'
> (*One Minute Wisdom*, New York, Doubleday, 1988, p. 125)

If that happens for even one of my readers, it will have been worth the effort.

A great many people have helped with this book. As part of the preparation for writing it I circulated some questions to a large number of would-be ordinands and lay people through the kind offices of a number of clergy. I am particularly grateful to the very many who were good enough to respond, some of them very fully and generously. If, here and there, they see their words quoted, I hope they will remember that I have done so because they succeeded in putting into words things that are true of more than just themselves, which, being shared, may become a mirror for others. I owe a great debt of gratitude also to those people who have talked to me in detail about aspects of their life and work and have allowed me to retell part of their stories for the benefit of my readers. It is not appropriate for me to mention their names, since in most cases they have been changed in order to preserve confidentiality. I am very grateful too to Mark Bryant, David Goodacre, John Greaves, Billy

Jackson, Anne Pemberton, Sister Rosemary CHN, Carol Simmons, John Skilbeck, Steve Walton, and David Wood who read through all or part of the first draft and made some most helpful and pertinent comments and suggestions; and also to Lindsey Ellin, who generously allowed me to use her account of her pre-theological college placement. I am especially indebted to Charles Richardson of the Advisory Board of Ministry of the Church of England with whom I discussed the whole project from the beginning and who has been unfailingly patient with my endless questions, and who also read through the first draft. None of these people should be held responsible for anything I have said. But I could not have done it at all without their assistance.

My very grateful thanks go also to Joan Trowbridge, whose speed and accuracy on the typewriter is only exceeded by her kindness in being willing to fit typing this book into an already very full life; and to Judith Longman of SPCK whose idea the whole thing was in the first place and whose evident confidence in me encouraged me to take on the task.

Inevitably my wife Elizabeth, and my children Bridget, Judith and Peter when they are at home, have borne the brunt of having to live with a pregnant author. They have done so with great grace and patience.

Francis Dewar
Durham
September 1990

Preface to the Second Edition

This book has really needed a second edition since it became possible for women to be ordained to the priesthood in the Church of England. While I was revising it, I came across these words of Charlotte Wolff: 'Women have always been the guardians of wisdom and humanity which makes them natural, but usually secret, rulers. The time has come for them to rule openly, but together with and not against men.' I would substitute 'guide' or 'lead' for 'rule' in the context of church life. I believe that, as far as the Anglican Church is concerned, what Charlotte Wolff hoped for is beginning to happen and that many people, even some who were at first doubtful, are finding that they very much appreciate the ministry of women priests. In the meantime, provision has also been made for those congregations and clergy who do not accept the ordination of women.

However, this book is addressed not just to people who are considering ordination, but to all women and men in the Anglican Church; and I venture to hope that it will be of use to members of other denominations, since the calling of God is addressed to all of us.

There is one other thing that needs to be said. The gender issue in our Church goes much further than the ordination of women. It concerns things like the use of inclusive language in our liturgies and in the translations of the Bible that we use. It extends, of course, to the language we use to speak about God. This is a sensitive question, on both sides of the divide, for those who are beginning to realize that there is an issue here – and for many who have not yet noticed that it is an issue. So I have only very gently approached this question in this edition, more simply to raise it than to answer it. It is a question we shall, as a Church, need to address more adequately before long.

In preparing this edition I was very grateful for some comments and suggestions by Mark Sowerby, the Vocations Adviser at Church House, and by Terry Nottage, the Diocesan Director of Ordinands for the diocese of Exeter.

Francis Dewar
Wells
January 2000

1

On Call

> There is an old Christian tradition
> that God sends each person into this
> world
> with a special message to deliver,
> with a special song to sing for others,
> with a special act of love to bestow.
> No one else can speak my message,
> or sing my song,
> or offer my act of love.
> These are entrusted only to me.

So writes John Powell (*Through Seasons of the Heart*, Collins 1988). This is your calling, your personal vocation from God at each stage of your life. Expressing that message, singing that song, offering that act of love will not only bring you the most profound fulfilment: it will also be for the freeing or for the enrichment of others. This is God's calling to each of us, to unearth and to give our innermost treasure.

And there is always something about it that is peculiar to each individual. Whatever you do in response to this calling it will have about it something that is unique to you; it will not just be some recognized role or some task that you do simply to fulfil other people's expectations. It is something that is entrusted to you personally. Until you discover it and offer it, it will be unknown and unexpected. If you do not offer it, it will remain for ever unoffered. But if you do respond, whatever the problems or difficulties, you discover that you are doing what you were born for, and find in it a profound sense of rightness. You find that peace of God which passes all understanding.

I wonder if you thought I was speaking of ordination! It is amazing how often these deep and universal human longings for fulfilment in life and in action get focused on the ordained ministry.

1

It will be my first task in this first chapter to try to unravel why this happens; because when it does it *can* have quite destructive consequences.

It will help if at the outset we try and disentangle three different senses in which the words calling and vocation are used. First there is the general sense, the calling to be a Christian, to be a follower of Christ, and to become a member of his body, the Church. This is the sense in which, for example, St Paul normally uses it. God's call in this sense is addressed to everyone.

A second sense of the word refers to the call to a role. A role is essentially something defined by others. Most secular jobs are roles in this sense. There is a job description which tells you what you have to do and, often, how you are to set about it. Being a priest or minister is also a role. There is not usually anything as formal as a job description, at least not in parish work. That does not alter the fact that there are strong role expectations, as you quickly find if you as the incumbent see the task differently from the way your parish sees it. But the majority of people, apart from the clergy, would not think of themselves as called by God to the job they are paid for. The call to a role is not for everyone.

A third sense of the word refers to a person's unique or personal vocation, and this is the one I was talking about at the beginning of this chapter. Potentially this again is for everyone. By it I mean a task or activity engaged in for the love of it by which others may be enriched or released: something you do as a freely-chosen expression of your nature and energy, something that expresses the unique essence of yourself which God calls out from you to be a gift to others. This can, of course, be an aspect of the job you are paid for; or it might be something you do as a sideline. But, whatever its context, it will essentially be a voluntary initiative of your own, and not usually something required of you by others. It is something that you will feel as it were from within, as an inner urge or prompting.

I hope the first sense is clear enough. I don't propose to say anything more about that here. But more needs to be said about the other two. It is very important to understand the difference between them, even if there are sometimes circumstances when they overlap. Lack of clarity about the difference can cause a lot of pain and heartache, as I will explain later.

The second sense in which the word vocation is used is in

connection with the calling to a role. It is vital to grasp that in this sense of the word the call comes through other people and is to a job or task that is defined by other people. In this sense, for example, there is the call, made to an individual by representatives of the Christian community, to accept appointment to a specific office required by the community for its well-being and its proper functioning. Ordination is a calling in this sense, where the calling of God is mediated through the community, the Church. To become a parson you don't just decide one day to put up a brass plate outside your door saying VICAR, however much you may be convinced in your own mind that that is what God wants you to be. There is a careful selection process by the official representatives of the Church to determine whether or not you have the right qualities for the job. (I will go into what these qualities are in chapter 6). A broadly similar process is involved in being appointed to any job. The firm or organization who wants a particular task doing interviews applicants and appoints the person most able to do what is required. Where this is a secular organization most people would be hesitant about claiming that *God* had called them to this job, least of all the organization itself. But where a person's individual gifts are very fully engaged and stretched by such a job, that person might well privately feel that it was something they were called by God to do. In this case it would be an example of something more akin to the third sense of the word calling. But most people do not feel identified to that extent with the work by which they earn their bread and butter.

It is about the third sense that there is the least awareness. It tends not to be recognized at all, either by the individual concerned, or by the Church, or by society in general. It is not recognized by individuals, at least with their minds, because it is usually pretty hidden and non-standard and difficult to discover. But our hearts know about it all right, if we give them half an ear. It is this that gives rise to all those nameless longings that often surface in people in their thirties or forties. In a slightly more explicit form it appears in the vague sense that 'God has something special for me to do' or 'God has something more for me to do' that so easily gets focused on ordination. It is not recognized by the Church because vocations are still largely thought of as what clergy or monks or nuns or missionaries have: and by implication the rest of us do not, whatever high-minded things may sometimes be proclaimed from pulpits. It is not acknowledged by society in general because to the public 'vocation' means certain kinds of professions, like doctor or nurse or teacher. Nowadays the phrase 'vocational training' obscures the issue even further. It usually means little more than 'teaching them what they need to fit them into what the job market requires'. It is more and more a case of producing persons for pigeonholes, and less and less about developing young people's creativity or originality. So to redress this lack of recognition and to do justice to this third sense we will need to give it a good deal of emphasis. We will come back to it in a moment.

I hope this helps to make the notion of calling or vocation a little clearer. The third sense is the one I intended at the beginning of this chapter, and is the one that will probably be least familiar. In fact it is probably so unfamiliar to make a distinction between the second and third senses that later on (in chapters 2 and 3) I shall explain more fully what I mean by personal vocation. For now I will explain the idea briefly, but I hope enough for you to begin to see why it is relevant in understanding the call to ordination. It is, of course, important for every Christian, and not just those who are ordained. So even if you personally are not considering ordination, I hope you will find that the notion of personal vocation illuminates your own living of the Christian life.

PERSONAL CALLING

I believe that potentially every human being has something of value to offer to the world's life. Many people would be surprised if you told them that. They would not think they had anything of value to offer at all. What society communicates to many is that they are of no worth except as cogs in a (sometimes) inhuman machine, the world of work, which requires slaves in order to function, but has no real regard for their development as persons with latent creative possibilities. Not everyone feels like this about work, of course, and the more middle-class you are probably the less you will see it this way. But it is true for a very large number of people, and if you are eventually ordained and perhaps work in a housing estate or an inner city district you will maybe understand more clearly what I mean. I myself believe that within every human being, at all levels of society, lie all kinds of undeveloped creative potential. That does not mean that everyone has a symphony up their sleeve or a novel in their back-pocket. We usually think of gifts and creativity in much too purple terms. I am thinking of much more ordinary capacities like the ability to listen, or to be playful, or to organize. God calls out from us all kinds of very 'ordinary' capacities like that so that in exercising them in a particular way among particular people they become gifts to others – or, perhaps more accurately, in the exercise of them we ourselves become a gift to others: because essentially it is ourselves that we give in what we do in this way. It is as in response to the inner nudgings of God we take the risk of doing things we are not required to do and taking initiatives unasked that it may become appropriate to use the language of personal calling. It does not have to be some lifelong, heroic step like Albert Schweitzer going to Lambaréné. It might just be something like offering to re-decorate an elderly couple's living room because actually you love messing about with wallpaper and paint, and risking the possibility that your offer may be rebuffed.

But most of our potential creativity and love remains hidden because we do not expect it. We do not expect it of ourselves, and we do not expect it of others. We fit ourselves comfortably within the safety of others' or society's expectations. We do not believe in *ourselves* enough for God to call out our treasures from us: and we do not believe in *God* enough to expect and to receive the Kingdom promised to us. Most of the time we dutifully and conscientiously do what is expected or demanded of us in accordance with our perceived place within the scheme of things. In short our expecta-tions of God and of ourselves fall short of God's glory. We perish in our dullness and others perish because of it.

Let me sum up this brief preliminary outline with a rough and ready list of some typical features of personal calling:

It will be some activity that connects deeply with your nature, character and history.
It will always be prompted by God.
There will be something new, creative and non-standard about it
  – perhaps never done before, or not in that particular way.
It often (perhaps usually) stems from some 'thorn in the flesh' that you have come to some sort of terms with, something you think

of as a problem, trauma or disaster, some wound, disability or handicap.

It will be something that in *some* way enriches the impoverished,
  or gives sight to the blind,
  or release to prisoners,
  or freedom for the oppressed.
  (I use these categories, from Luke 4.18–19, in a very wide sense indeed.)

You will be doing what in your heart of hearts you love to do (even if it brings you hassle and trouble, even suffering).

It will be an initiative that *you* take, probably unasked, one that will not be taken unless you do it.

It will feel risky, something you would only do because you feel God has called you to (and you have checked with one or two wise and spiritually mature Christians that it is God, and not just your ego!).

It will always be a generous self-giving of what you truly are and could be.

It will, in some way or other, somewhere along the line, prove personally costly for you.

It is more likely, statistically speaking, to be in the secular sphere than in the Church, simply because there is more of it!

It is unlikely to be lifelong, or full time, or paid – it is more likely to be something you do from time to time, or for short periods, in your own time. But, if you respond, it will become a thread that runs through more and more of your life.

If it is at work, it will be something you do beyond the requirements of the job description (and it may get you into hot water). Or it may be expressed in the *way* in which you fulfil some part of the job description.

I hope I have managed to explain, if only in outline at this stage, that God's personal calling is to an *infinite* variety of activities. Not only will the activities themselves be varied, but also the amount of time and energy they require: so also will the context vary, e.g. it may be something you do at work or in your spare time, in the Church or in the world, in the public sphere or privately and unseen, individually or with others, and so on. This variety is to be expected when you reflect on the fact that it is God who calls and that there is always something new and unexpected about what God calls us to.

I want to say a little more now about how and why it is that an inner sense of being called by God so easily gets attached to ordination; in other words how the second and third senses of the word calling so easily get confused. There are basically two reasons: one is because of the nature of work in our society and the effects it has had on all of us in the past two centuries; the other is because of the Church's own muddled ideas about vocation.

THE NATURE OF WORK IN OUR SOCIETY AND ITS EFFECTS

We live in a society where work is almost entirely defined by others. One of the effects of the industrial revolution was to increase this alienation between what we are and what we do. Jobs for most people are defined by the requirements of a process, whether that be making cars or cakes, selling insurance or package holidays. Scope for genuinely creative activity is either non-existent or severely constrained by the requirement that the company you work for must produce goods or services that are saleable at a profit or it will go to the wall. This feature about the nature of work in the modern world has sunk deep into our consciousness, so deep that it affects our activities outside the sphere of paid work. Many of us can hardly conceive what our daily activity would be if it were not demanded of us, expected of us, or at least asked of us by someone else. In other words, a very great deal of our life is lived in response to outside stimuli, instead of from within outwards.

I believe this factor is one of the reasons why, when prompted by an inner sense of call, we go for a ready-made niche, as it were. The ordained ministry is there as a handy receptacle which feels as though it will accommodate our vague longings and give some shape to them. If you ask people, as I have done, why they want to be ordained, their ideas are often very vague and quite unfocused. 'I want to learn more of my faith so that I can share it.' 'I feel God is calling me to something more.' 'I want to enter into a deeper commitment to people.' Or simply 'I want to grow closer to God.' Looking at these reasons it is not at all clear that ordination is the only or the obvious course of action. Sometimes people recognize this; one person wrote, 'For me the call to serve was crystal clear; but the question of ordination specifically was not spelled out.'

7

It is not that these people do not have a call of some kind. They clearly do, and are beginning to hear echoes of it. But what they are hearing is, I believe, usually the echo of a personal call from God that, so to speak, gets reflected from the bulwarks of the ordained ministry. There, after all, is the most obvious public model and pattern of a committed and dedicated Christian life. A dedicated and committed Christian life is potentially what God calls every one of us to. But, as I said at the beginning of this chapter, it is much more personal and idiosyncratic than a predetermined role like ordination. You are called by him to deliver *your* message, to sing *your* song, to offer *your* act of love: and that is not a predetermined path. As you respond, God calls you on. As you respond, God calls you ever further and further into being the gift you could be. That is, after all, how we are to follow Christ; we are to be generous with what we are and could be, just as he was generous with what he was. We are called to total self-giving as he was, but each of us *in our own way* and not in some predetermined standardized path. (I have explained this in relation to Jesus more fully in chapter 6 of my book *Live for a Change*.)

THE CHURCH'S MUDDLED IDEAS ABOUT VOCATION

These have certainly contributed in the minds of most church people to a fundamental confusion between the calling to a role (the second sense) and personal calling (the third sense). If it is not yet clear to you that there is any confusion, let me put it like this. Suppose you feel called to be ordained; and you go to a bishops' selection conference and you are not recommended. That happens quite often: and when it does, who has got it wrong? The selectors? Or you? Or God?

It could be that the selectors got it wrong; but they do take a great deal of care and trouble at selection conferences. No one is infallible, of course, but I find it difficult to believe that they get it wrong every time someone is 'not recommended'.

Did you get it wrong? Were you simply mistaken in thinking that God is calling you? I think it is both unfair and cruel to load all responsibility for error on to the candidate. As I have begun to explain, I think that the candidate's error is usually not that they are

8

not being called, but in assuming too hastily that the call is to ordination.

Did God get it wrong, then? I suppose the only answer to that is that none of us is infallibly privy to the mind of God. Is it possible that God keeps getting it wrong? I think it is more likely that somewhere or other *we* have got it wrong, and by us I do not mean any particular individual, I mean the Church as a whole. In other words I personally think it is only because of the Church's muddled ideas about vocation that these pained questions come to be asked at all. Basically the Church does not see any difference between the second and third senses of the word calling. That is where the confusion lies.

Let me try and explain how this muddle has come about. If you look at the Anglican ordination service in *The Book of Common Prayer*, you will see that prospective deacons are asked: 'Do you trust that you are *inwardly moved by the Holy Ghost* to take upon you this office and ministration ... ?' Candidates for the priesthood are asked: 'Do you think *in your own heart* that you be truly called ... ?' *The Alternative Service Book 1980* requires a bishop to ask a similar question of prospective deacons and priests: 'Do you believe, *as far as you know your own heart*, that God has called you to the office and work of a deacon/priest in his Church?' (Italics mine.)

Anything that appears in print must be right, you might think: and if it appears printed in a church prayerbook as words for a bishop to say, then who can possibly argue with it? Well, church historians can, and they do. The fact is that the requirement that a candidate for the priesthood should have an inner sense of calling to that office is relatively recent in the history of the Church. Questions probing the candidate's inner sense of calling do not appear in church ordinals before the sixteenth century. Their appearance on the scene was a symptom of some radical changes in the notion of ordained ministry that had gradually taken place since the early days of the Christian Church. A very clear exponent of these changes is Edward Schillebeeckx, for example, in his book *Ministry, A Case for Change* (SCM 1981). He points out that in the first ten centuries of the Church's history, it was the local Christian community that had the chief part to play in the choice of its leader. In fact, the Council of Chalcedon in 451 forbade 'absolute' ordinations. In other words, in no way was ordination to be regarded as the bestowal of some special power, to be your personal possession for the rest of your life. On the contrary, it was simply your appointment and election as the leader in your local Christian community. You could not be ordained unless you had been asked by a particular Christian community to be its leader. Conversely, if you ceased to be the president of your community, you automatically became a layman again. In other words ordination was linked entirely with the person's function within the Christian community.

By the medieval period there had come a change; the influence of secular ideas from the Roman legal system had given rise to the notion that the power assigned to the priest/leader of the Christian community came not from the community which he served but resided within himself as a 'sacred power' bestowed on him at ordination, precisely what the Council of Chalcedon had forbidden. The rise of feudalism also contributed to this, where clergy became the servants of secular lords instead of congregations. Schillebeeckx' book is very clear and very readable, and should be read by every aspiring ordinand.

So you see, in the early centuries of the Church, clergy were leaders drawn from the communities where they were to serve and in whose choice the community had a big say. Whether a person chosen in this way had an inward sense of calling to be a church leader was neither here nor there. The job needed doing, and if a person was chosen as suitable by the church community that person was expected to comply. There are many famous examples of church leaders who not only had no inner sense of call but resisted being appointed, for example St Ambrose, St Martin of Tours, and St Augustine. Gregory Dix writes: 'The early Church thrust Holy Orders on many who were most sincerely reluctant to receive them, and refused many who were strongly conscious of their call to the episcopate' (A. G. Hebert, ed., *The Parish Communion*, SPCK 1957, p. 130). Traces of this earlier attitude to ordination survive today in the Eastern Orthodox Church where the candidate for the diaconate or the priesthood is led forward to be ordained by two clergy who hold him by the arms – in case he tries to escape!

Now you may say that just because it was done in this way in the early Church is insufficient reason for doing it this way now. I grant you that: but I would add that if the way we do it now is actually a bit of a nonsense, although we have been doing it that way for a few centuries, that is no good reason for continuing.

Leaving aside for a moment the historical questions, look at it from a common sense point of view. Every institution needs leaders, and the Church is no exception. The most basic function of the leader in any community or institution is to keep it true to its nature. That is, to prevent it turning into something else. Suppose the chairman of the local choral society is secretly keen on drama. He suggests that next year instead of *Messiah* they will do *The Marriage of Figaro* – just a concert performance, he assures them. But the members are not fools and they know perfectly well that opera is not what they are there to sing; and they are rightly incensed. He gets his drama all right, at the very next annual meeting. He is voted out with much acrimony.

Now where you have a situation, as we do in the Church of England, where leaders cannot be voted in or out, it is very important that the people chosen as leaders have the right qualities for the job (see chapter 6). That is the over-riding requirement. And usually other people are in a better position to judge what qualities a candidate has, rather than the candidate himself or herself. So, simply looking at it from a common sense point of view suggests that an inner sense of calling to the job is not going to be high on the list of required qualities. Presently, I shall argue that an inner sense of calling is important, but not quite in the way that is usually assumed.

In 1938 H. L. Goudge wrote:

> The first question put to those to be ordained to the Diaconate in the Anglican Ordinal – 'Do you trust that you are inwardly called by the Holy Ghost to take upon you this office and ministration . . . ?' – is nothing less than a disaster. It has probably lost to the ministry hundreds of men who might have made admirable clergy; and it tends to cause painful searchings of heart in times of depression to many rightly ordained. A good meaning can be attached to the question, but what it suggests is the necessity for a strong sense of vocation, as in the case of an Old Testament prophet.

He explains that the enquiry about inward call appears in the Ordinal because:

> Our Reformers, misled by Martin Bucer, confused the regular with the prophetic ministry. The position of prophets does largely rest upon their

11

inward call. The Church . . . recognises their position and discriminates
between true prophecy and false; but it does no more than this. But the
position of the regular ministers, who may have no remarkable gifts,
depends upon their ordination and commission by the Apostles, and it is
for others to judge of their suitability rather than for themselves. They
must believe that they are doing the will of God in what they do, and
must keep back nothing which those who ordain ought to know; but
Scripture does not justify us in asking more than this, nor does any
Church Ordinal earlier than the sixteenth century.

(*The Church of England and Reunion*, SPCK 1938, p. 181, quoted by
Kenneth Noakes in an essay in *Ministers of the Kingdom*, CIO 1985)

I hope that this will have helped to explain how the Church's
confusion between an inner sense of calling and the calling to the
role of ordained person came about. Goudge's distinction between
the regular and the prophetic ministry is a helpful one. It
corresponds to the second and third senses of the word calling. Many
people think of a prophet in narrowly and superficially Old
Testament terms as someone very unusual and very high-powered
and often very dogmatic, and moreover someone who *says* things,
usually of the 'thus saith the Lord . . .' variety. It is easy to get that
impression from the Old Testament. We will come back to this again
in chapter 5. But I personally find myself very much in sympathy
with Moses when he said 'Would that all the Lord's people were
prophets'. By which I mean that I long for the day when every
Christian lives her/his personal response to God's calling. And of
course many do. That is what it would mean for all the Lord's
people to be prophets. What a marvellously rich and creative
contribution we would make to the life of the world! Each person
would be living their personal unusualness and creativity in meeting
the needs and problems and opportunities of the world today, not
out of some heavy sense of 'ought' but with the deep joy that comes
from doing what God has made you for and what he personally calls
you to. Each person would be responsive to God as themselves, and
not in some second-hand, imitative way. In John Powell's metaphor,
each of us would be singing his song, embodying her message,
bestowing our love.

That, as I understand it, is what it is to be a prophet. And it is
entirely appropriate that we hear God's call to this as an inner sense
of calling. It is the secret silent voice of God in the depths of our
being prompting us to give of our innermost treasure in some

particular task. It is important, as Goudge suggested, that the Church should have some say in judging whether this calling is genuine or not, and we do not at present have the mechanism for this in the Anglican Church. (The Quakers do, though, and we could learn much from them – see my *Live for a Change*, 2nd edn, p. 132.) But it should not be confused with the calling to ordination.

THE FUNCTION OF THE ORDAINED LEADER

It may be that it is not yet clear to you that this is basically a role, that is to say a function defined by others in accordance with the needs of the Christian community. Maybe you had secretly hoped it was a licence to do your own thing, complete with a free house and an assured income for life! I think it can sometimes look like that, and is occasionally treated like that by its occupants. At present the great diversity of tasks engaged in by ordained people does certainly blur their function. We are, after all, in a time of experiment and ferment about the nature of ministry. But, as I shall explain more fully later, I believe that we shall understand the nature of the ordained ministry more clearly a) when we understand better the nature of what it is to be a lay person – a member of the laos (the people of God) – and b) when we can see it as ordained-ministry-in-community, i.e. not divorced from its clear function in the Christian community.

Basically what is required of the ordained person is to keep the Christian community true to what it is, to prevent it turning into a Masonic club, or a social work agency, or a political party, or what have you. The tasks this requirement dictates are things like teaching, leading worship, and modelling the Christian life. These are the basic duties for which the Church needs candidates. From day to day the work of a parish priest can involve all kinds of less high-sounding activities. A friend who is a nun wrote, 'I suspect that most lay people think first about leading worship and giving personal guidance; I know that until I started working in a parish I had no idea of the time clergy had to spend on administration, finance, meetings, buildings, putting in an appearance at local events, schools, production-line occasional offices, etc. It made me very thankful *not* to be a cleric!'

A person chosen for the ordained ministry does not need an

inward sense of vocation to the basic task. What he or she does need are the right qualities for it. That is why the choice needs to be made by others, by the duly appointed representatives of the institution. The Church in effect says to a person, 'You are called by God to be ordained'. Thus the calling of God needs to come, not on a personal hotline from God, but via the Church. In practice it often comes in the first place through the suggestion of the vicar, or of friends, or of other people in the congregation. But this will need to be checked by the Church's selection process and eventually the Church's choice will be formally expressed in the ordination service.

When it comes to doing the job you may or may not feel an inner sense of calling to it, or you may feel it to some parts of the job and not to others. But there is a sense in which whether you feel that or not is irrelevant. There is no reason why you should not, but it is not *required*. That is to say, it is not required that you feel an inner sense of calling *to the particular tasks to be done by a cleric*.

THE IMPORTANCE OF THE ORDAINED LEADER RESPONDING TO GOD'S PERSONAL CALL

But if you are ordained you do need an inner sense of vocation in *some* aspect of your activities. I believe it is essential that candidates for ordination should be people who are consciously responding to God's personal call to them in some area of their life. It might be in some task outside anything remotely resembling ministerial or priestly activity: or it might be in some part of the vicar's job. What is essential for such candidates is that they have begun to discover their personal calling in the third sense I described earlier. I believe that to be a basic requirement for any Christian. Therefore the vicar needs to be living his or her response to God's personal calling *because (s)he is a Christian*, and not just because (s)he is ordained. His or her living of it as an ordained person is part of a vicar's modelling of a Christian life that is for everyone. So, for example, if the vicar's personal vocation is spending time outside the parish with homeless young people and seeking with them a way out of their difficulties, (s)he will do that as a private individual, not because (s)he is vicar of a parish. In fact some of the parishioners may not be too keen on the vicar spending a lot of time outside the parish. After all, contrary to what some clergy think, being a cleric does not give him or her *carte blanche* to do their own thing regardless: (s)he will have to explain what (s)he does and why (s)he does this task. In doing so, if (s)he is truly called, there will shine out from him or her love and enthusiasm and giftedness for this work. (S)he will be modelling a style of life and activity that should be part of every Christian's existence.

For would-be clergy – and even though what I am saying is true for all, I have them primarily in mind in what I am saying at this point – I believe it to be essential that your sense of God's personal and unique calling to you develops. This is necessary for two reasons. First, one of the dangers that particularly beset the clergy is over-identification with the role often to the point of self-parody. But the fact is that no one is role-shaped. No one exactly fits a role: and no role gives expression to the whole of what a person could be. You have to adapt yourself in order to fill a role. There is nothing wrong with that. You have to in order to be able to fulfil its requirements; and society and its institutions simply could not function without roles. They are essential to common life. What is damaging is when people are persuaded that they *are* the role, that there is nothing in them that is not the role. This begins to destroy their humanity. Clergy who are tempted to this can be a destructive and de-humanizing influence in their congregations.

The second reason why it is necessary that you grow in your response to God's unique calling to you is because it is important that your response to God in action is a personal one and not just a standardized one. Look at it this way: if it is important that each of us has a personal relationship with God in prayer, it is also necessary that our response to God in action is in some respects our own and not just an other-determined one.

Let me illustrate what I mean from my own ministry. When I first became vicar of a parish I found the going pretty rough. The parish situation I inherited was not an easy one. It was a recently formed parish and there were a number of difficult issues which had been ducked by the previous regime which were obviously going to need to be faced, and it would probably take several years to deal with them. There were times in the first three or four years when I wondered if perhaps my function was simply to be the catalyst to break the situation open, so that someone else could follow and be able to do some creative work with the congregation. I felt there was very little that I could do in that way at that stage.

There was also the fact that the change from being an assistant to being an incumbent is not always an easy one. As a vicar you carry the can in a way that an assistant does not. And in my day there were no courses for first incumbents. You just sank or swam. I didn't sink, but I did find it very hard going. Fulfilling the role of ordained leader for me at that stage in that parish was a painful business. To preserve some sense of worthwhileness in my ministry I began to run courses outside the parish in counselling, which was one of my interests at the time. As time went by and we began to face the problems in the parish I began to be able to use my gift for teaching adults within the parish. My gift is not so much for counselling as for teaching, for enabling people to learn. It began to be possible to use this in, for example, the adult confirmation classes. I began to find the courage to design my own confirmation course in a somewhat non-standard way. Gradually this spread to other areas of the church's life. We began to have parish weekends away and other extra-curricular activities. I began to feel a great sense of personal satisfaction in this part of the work, and it was evidently valued by people who came within its influence. In fact it was because of people's reactions that I began to realize that I had any gift for this at all. I had discovered a part of the role, or it had discovered me, in which I was able to offer my own God-given gift in a full-blooded way. I was fortunate in that in the end (though it was not so at the beginning) God's personal calling to me for that stage of my life was related to a recognized part of the clerical role. If you are ordained, it does help when that happens, but it is not guaranteed. God's personal calling to you may well be outside anything recognizable as part of a vicar's job.

As far as the clergy are concerned, the relative proportion of role or idiosyncrasy, of priest or prophet, in their activities will obviously vary enormously. But I hope I have said enough to make it clear that it is important that both find a place. It is of vital importance that we keep some sort of balance between chore activities and joy activities. This is not just to preserve the humanity of the parson, but also the health of the congregation.

The reason why this affects the health of the congregation is twofold. If the vicar is not finding fulfilment by exercising his gift, his particularity, his personal call, he will tend to prevent others doing so. There is a sort of dog-in-the-manger dynamic that operates when a person is not, at least in some aspects of their life, doing what they are made for. There is always envy skulking around in such a person. It may cause them, whether they are aware of it or not, to resent or even hinder other people finding and responding to their personal vocation. For example, in the diocese of Durham there is an Arts and Recreation Chaplain. It is a unique ministry that developed out of the gifts of the person who does this work. Soon after his appointment a certain clergyman was heard to remark acidly, 'I suppose we'll be having a chaplain to the model railway club next!'

Secondly, if the incumbent is responding to God's personal call to her, it will enable her to sit lighter to the role aspects of the ministry, and allow opportunities for others in the congregation to share some of the role duties where appropriate. If she is not following her personal call, she will be over-identified with the role and may feel that she has got to be the king-pin in every parish activity. This does not make for servant leadership!

I hope I have now said enough about the second and third senses of the word vocation to enable you to begin to see the difference. It is very important to distinguish between them. Much damage can be done when features appropriate to one are attributed to the other; for instance when it is assumed that people should have an inward sense of calling to be a parson/church leader. Many clergy who conscientiously soldier on in the middle or later years of their ministries without much sense of joy in what they do need to be reassured that they are not required to feel that their ministry must be the be-all and end-all of their life. Many in their heart of hearts do not feel it is, but think they ought to feel it and are weighed down by that thought.

Equally we need to move away from the notion that the feeling that one does have a sense of calling to be ordained automatically qualifies one for the role of the ordained minister. It does not, and it would save a lot of unnecessary heartache for 'not recommended' candidates if the Church were clearer about that.

I hope you have also understood my insistence that every ordained person needs to be living *some* aspect of his or her life in response to God's personal call. This is, or ought to be, a vital dimension of what it is to be a Christian, and the clergy should be fully Christian in this way. When the ACCM (now the Ministry Division of the Archbishops' Council) report *Call To Order* appeared in 1989 it espoused the threefold understanding of vocation that I have outlined and made some recommendations to the Church on the basis of that. However, the way their message was received by many made it look as though the report was saying, 'Clergy should be recruited, like civil servants. An inward sense of calling is not required.' I hope it is now clear that what both they and I are trying to say is a little more subtle than newspaper headlines will allow. A response to an inward sense of calling *is* required – i.e. candidates for ordination should have some experience of responding to an inner sense of call in some area of their life. But what is not required is an inner sense of call to ordination.

HOW THE IDEA OF ORDINATION COMES TO PEOPLE AND IS PERCEIVED BY THEM

It may be that you are still basically unconvinced by what I am saying in this first chapter. You may point to your inner sense of call and say to me, 'You are wrong. I have the clearest possible personal sense that God is calling me to be ordained.' Many people have said that to me in one way or another. I think for example of Trevor. He told me, 'Jesus woke me up in the middle of the night and said "I want you to be a priest".' He was nineteen at the time. Two or three years before, the choirmaster at his church had suggested the possibility of ordination after he had been to a youth club praise evening at Trevor's invitation. But at that time Trevor had not been disposed to take the suggestion seriously.

For David, the idea of ordination came within days of discovering the Church. 'Although I understood very little of what was involved at the time, it was as if I understood what my life was for.' For Mark, it came 'overwhelmingly' as a result of 'the experience of a single event where I felt unmistakably drawn to offer my life in full-time service'.

For Margaret, it seemed to appear 'out of the blue. I first started thinking about ordination three or four years ago. But at the time it was only a very vague idea which I did not take seriously.' It was similar for Karen:

> This call seemed to come completely out of the blue shortly before I was confirmed in June. But with hindsight I can see that it entered my consciousness in an undefined form as I emerged from a spiritual

conversion experience at the beginning of February. During this period there was an occasion when I found myself seeking solitude by the river, feeling angry at God, protesting against the fact that he had called me to Christ as a silly little island in the middle of a sea of atheism, cutting me off from everything and everybody I knew. As so often happened during such an emotional display on my part, there was a sudden unexpected silence, almost audible, as though everything was aware that God would enter. And immediately I was taken over by a deep wish to be ordained. It must have been evening and pitch dark, because it was a public footpath and I can remember falling to my knees and praying fervently that God might use me in this way. I did not know anything about ordination. I wasn't even aware that I knew the word. And I put the whole thing to the back of my mind, dismissing the incident as an emotional outburst.

Others approach it more rationally. Asked, 'What gave you the idea of ordination?' Joan said: 'On the one hand, reading and thinking a good deal about the issue of women's ordination as a theological question; on the other hand searching and praying to know what I myself should be doing to live out my faith. At some point these two threads joined together. Being at a church with a deaconess who was ordained deacon at about that time brought the matter closer to home and made it a conceivable path.'

For many people, what draws them is a desire for more whole-hearted discipleship. 'It is a life, not merely a job confined to particular hours or tasks,' said one. Another wrote: 'I do not want to divide my life into a nine to five job to earn my living and then cram my vocation into "spare" time.' And another: 'I feel it would free me to fulfil more fully the role of praying and listening that I am at present exercising in my church.' And so on.

In these various examples you can perhaps discern the basic human search for fulfilment and for God that underlies what all of them say in one way or another. God is always drawing us on to move from where we are towards him. That is true of our prayer life. It is also true of our active life. It may be that for some of these people, if they are in the end ordained, the clerical role will provide greater freedom to exercise God's calling to them. But the expectation that it will *can* be an illusion. Strange as it may seem, many older clergy I have spoken to find it just as difficult to discover and respond to God's personal calling to them as any nine to five wage slave. For example, a friend who has been in parish ministry for thirty years wrote: 'I have felt, since I was about eighteen, that I would like to be a composer. Apart from sporadic outbursts, I have had to suppress it all, because of the amount of time it would involve. I could do it if I were a lay Christian, but not as a priest.'

What seems to happen in practice is that, though there is less outer constraint for a vicar – usually you have a good deal of freedom to organize your own work schedule – there are in practice considerable inner constraints that cause many clergy to be conscientious to the point of workaholism. The personal calling element gets crowded out by the dictates of a misguided conscience, a kind of drivenness caused partly by internalizing the unreasonable expectations of parishioners and partly by the open-endedness of the job – there is *always* more to do than it is possible to do.

So I understand the strength of your inner sense of calling. I experience it myself at times, and it is vital to work with it, to discern what God is asking of you, and to respond. Your life and your liveliness depend on it. But do understand that in God's personal calling to you you are not handed a life plan on a plate. When David said, 'it was as if I understood what my life was for,' he was no doubt thinking, 'My life's work is to be a parson.' But what he actually said was, 'it was as *if* I understood . . .' He was accurately, perhaps more accurately than he realized, describing the inner sense of rightness that usually goes with beginning to respond to God's personal call. But in fact 'what my life is for' changes and develops as I respond to God. My response in action can only be said to be what my life is for at one stage of my life at a time. There is nothing permanent about it. As they say at Taizé, '*tout est provisoire*,' everything is provisional, especially in the sphere of personal calling.

So if you have a growing inner sense of calling of any kind from God, it is important to act upon it; but one step at a time. As you do so God will call you on further: but never assume you can see more than a step or two ahead. God is nothing if not unexpected. That is true of the God we encounter in the Bible, and I certainly have found it to be true in my own life and in the lives of others I have met.

So if you are convinced that God is calling you to offer yourself for ordination, by all means consult with other godly and perceptive people; and if it seems right, begin to explore with your Diocesan Director of Ordinands the possibility of going to a selection conference. But at each stage be ready for the unexpectedness of God. *As far as whether you are to be ordained or not is concerned, that call will* come through the appointed representatives of God's Church. As far as God's personal calling to you is concerned, that will be something that you sense primarily within, although you will need to check it with others.

There is one other group of reasons for wanting to be ordained which I perhaps need to mention. Quite often people seek ordination because they are looking for 'affirmation' or 'confidence' or 'authority'. This actually seems to cover quite a wide spectrum of motivation. At one end of the spectrum is Pat. When she went to a selection conference, she was asked why she wanted to be ordained: 'I told them I wanted to carry with me some authority and status, something I could carry on my own without resorting to my husband, in whose shadow I had spent most of my life hitherto. All I wanted was to be recognized as someone with something to offer, separate from my husband. Training would give me the confidence I needed. It would help me to be a better Christian, understand my faith better, and help me to share it more widely.' What Pat was looking for primarily was to be recognized as a person in her own right. If she had been ordained the chances are that the person she could become would have been even more effectively swamped. But I do sympathize with her desire for Christian learning. That is a very common reason why people offer themselves for ordination. They see it as the only way to get a proper theological training. And let's face it, more of the Church's educational resources are spent on training one clergyman than a hundred lay people.

At the other end of the spectrum is John, a software engineer in a large company:

> It is my belief that the laity need desperately some church leadership which actually leads the life they lead themselves; not people who will supply the answers, but who at least have some understanding of the questions. That church leadership has to be ordained. I don't believe in ordination; but it is a fact with which we have to deal. People recognize its authority. (If I say fornication is to be encouraged, it's just me talking. If the Vicar of Bray says it, there's an outcry . . .) In addition, it is only through the representations of fellow clergy that the Church will ever take seriously the issues and dilemmas faced by lay people at work.

John has in fact offered himself for ordination as a Non-stipendiary Minister (NSM) but he sees the issue as much wider than a personal one for him; it is about how the Church almost completely fails to understand or support what Christians do in their secular place of work.

This is a *cri de coeur* with which I have much sympathy. Mostly the Church does not recognize what people do at work or in secular contexts as ministry at all. But I have to say that I am not convinced that actually *ordaining* people all over the place is the answer, at least not in the long run. Taken to its logical conclusion, that would seem to me to require that every mature Christian should receive some kind of 'ordination to daily work'. I can see a lot of good sense in the substance of that (see my *Live for a Change*, 2nd edn, p. 181), but to call it ordination only confuses the issue. I think, as things are at present, John is right about the occasional need for ordained people in work situations, for the practical reasons he gives. But I have to say that, theologically, it is a bit of a nonsense, as will be clear from what I have been saying up to now. What we really need is a far stronger and more full-blooded sense of what it means to be a Christian lay person. And that requires a much more thorough-going training than most lay people receive.

In between these opposite ends of the spectrum are those who think the collar will provide recognition of who they are and 'access to people's lives in ways not open to a lay person'. Well, it can. But the collar can also be a barrier dividing you from people. To take a trivial example, I remember once as a parish priest doing some visiting of new arrivals on a council estate. It was evening. The wife answered the door and, yes, she invited me in; but as she did so I noticed the husband surreptitiously hiding the glass of beer he was drinking. It just *could* have been that it was his last pint, and that he wasn't in a position to offer me one. It is much more likely that he thought I stood for a number of 'thou shalt nots'!

Inevitably in these pages I am having to write in relation to the way things are in the Church of England, and not just the way things might be. When I wrote the first edition of this book, women were not allowed to be priests in the Church of England. It therefore seemed appropriate to say a specific word to those women who wanted to be ordained. At that time I felt that when a woman became aware of an inner sense of call to be ordained it had a different feel about it in a Church where ordination to the priesthood was not open to them. The call to ordination that at least some of them felt within themselves was *not* an example of the muddle between the second and third senses of the word vocation (see pp. 8ff). There was a genuinely prophetic element in it. Many women felt a call not just to be ordained, but to *change* the way the ordained ministry is to be exercised. One of the ordinands who was kind enough to reply to my questionnaire wrote, 'I feel [being an ordinand] is a right offering to make to the Church, especially because I am a woman; and I believe that the inclusion of women in the ranks of the ordained clergy will change the nature of the ordained role for the better.'

In other words, for many women at that time there was a strong element of personal calling in their desire to be ordained. I think that that may still be the case for some, not least because the fact that women can now be priests does not guarantee the wholehearted acceptance of their ministry. There can still be quite strong discouragements to the ministry of women in the Church.

There can also be discouragements for people from a working-class background seeking ordination. A friend whose background is solidly working-class went through the whole gamut of selection and training and was ordained in 1989. His impression was that middle-class assumptions permeated the whole process. He reckons that if you have been a manual worker and you find yourself in later years at theological college, there will be surprise in the minds of your fellow students at college if not actually on their lips – 'How on earth did you get here?' Rather like women in senior management positions, he believes that people from a working-class background need to prove themselves far beyond anything that is required of more 'expected' candidates. My friend's message to others in his position is, 'You'll have to work twice as hard to be accepted; you'll sometimes feel unsteady on your feet; but don't be put off.' E. R. Wickham (*Church and People in an Industrial City*, Lutterworth 1957) charted the yawning gulf between the Churches and working people that opened up as the industrialization of Britain got under way. It is a gulf that is still largely unbridged in the Church of England. However, I am assured that in the last few years selection conferences for those seeking ordination have incorporated features that are much better designed to help candidates from working-class backgrounds.

People whose skin is black can encounter even more discouragement. A priest friend who is black was a visiting preacher one Sunday in a multi-racial parish. Half the congregation was black, but all the clergy were white. They were obviously doing some very good work in the parish, but nevertheless when the preacher ascended the pulpit he could feel the lift in the mood of the congregation before he had said a single word, simply because the black members could see that here was a priest who was one of them.

Black people in this country feel undervalued and put down in all kinds of ways, subtle and not so subtle. The lack of role models is only one of the difficulties likely to face you as a black ordinand. When you go to a selection conference you will probably be the only black, and the same may well be the case at theological college. Moreover the approach to theology and ministry will put heavy emphasis on a rational and intellectual approach. Little if any emphasis will be placed on a theology which takes as its starting point the experience of individuals and peoples. 'I felt I had to leave a lot of myself behind,' said one black woman at theological college; 'even in the library there was hardly anything to help me make connections between the theology we were being taught and my own culture and background.' As the time of your ordination approaches, the question, 'Is there a place for me in the Church of England as a black?' will be more and more insistent, as you begin to wonder, 'Will it be difficult to find a parish for me?'

Black people who have been brought up as Anglicans all their lives often feel bewildered and hurt by being made to feel strangers in their own Church. Canon Sehon Goodridge who was brought up in the West Indies (he was principal of Codrington College, Barbados, for eleven years) and lived for a time in this country commented, 'The Church of England could do with a good dose of Anglicanism from Africa or the Caribbean.' He quotes from Arnold Toynbee's *A Study of History*: 'It is possible that the negro slave-immigrants who have found Christianity in America may perform the greater miracle of raising the dead to life ... they may perhaps be capable of rekindling the cold grey ashes of Christianity,' and expresses the hope that perhaps this is something our black sisters and brothers have to offer us here in Britain too. In 1990 he became the first principal of the Simon of Cyrene Theological Institute in South London (see Appendix p. 120) which has full financial backing from the Church of England. He feels that 'the time has come' for black Anglicans in this country; 'the Church is beginning to take us seriously, but it doesn't really know what to do with us.' The function of the Institute is to address this question and to grasp this opportunity. It is not a college. It has the much wider brief of articulating the mind and heart of black people in Britain and developing a theology which expresses shared black experience. It hopes to do this by running conferences and short courses for both blacks and whites around those questions. It will also offer a one year preparatory course for black ordinands before entry to the theological colleges and courses of their respective denominations, to enable them to understand and own their particular character, and to become secure in their personal identity as Christians and human beings.

The difficulties which may face you as a black ordinand will be considerable. Some black clergy would say that they have to prove themselves three times over to be accepted. You will be under tremendous scrutiny. But it is also a time of enormous opportunity which could bring great blessings both to blacks and whites in the Church of England.

2

A double invitation: 1

I explained in the last chapter that an inner sense of call is God nudging you towards something much more personal and idiosyncratic than a predetermined role, something that in the end will be nothing less than the discovery and subsequent offering of your true self. This is so little understood and of such fundamental importance that it will occupy this and the next three chapters. I will come back to the question of the role of the priest/minister in chapter 6.

The personal calling of God has two foci: to being, and to action. This is very obvious in the life and ministry of Jesus. All the gospellers in their different ways witness to the fact that everything Jesus said and did flowed from his close relationship with his Father. That closeness is the prime fact of his life and ministry. St John expresses it as a mutual indwelling or interpenetration of Jesus and the Father, 'I am in the Father and the Father in me' (14.10). The Gospels of Matthew, Mark and Luke describe it in terms of going apart to pray and spend time with his Father (e.g. Matt. 14.13; 14.23; Mark 6.46; Luke 9.18; Matt. 17.1–8; etc.) and give us brief glimpses of an intimacy (e.g. Mark 14.36) which is everywhere implied by Jesus' teaching and by the inherent authoritativeness of his way of living. As Gordon Cosby once put it in a sermon, 'From this intimacy flow his sense of his Father's constant presence, his sense of always being guided by him, his sense of timing, his empowering, his authority which was impressive even to his enemies, his freedom to break all the rules and conventions of his day, his courage to tackle the powers of death and darkness in the religious and political systems of his day, and finally in his willingness to be tortured and to die for us.'

We are invited to a similar level of intimacy with God (e.g. John 14.12; 15.1–16). God's personal calling to us is first and foremost to be with him; it is a call to being rather than doing; an invitation simply to be in God's presence. This is to be primary for us, as it was for Jesus. Only out of this stillness and being in God can we be genuinely responsive to the call to action. If what we do does not arise out of this stillness and waiting, it will have more to do with activism than called action. It will be action in our own strength, self-generated, and to a greater or lesser extent it will probably be in the service of our own ego. That is the way to burn-out, sooner or later.

In theory the importance of both prayer and action is well understood in the Church. In practice, because of the kind of society we live in which glorifies doing at the expense of being, prayer often gets turned into another kind of activity. We are tempted to measure it by its usefulness. We think of it as intercession, getting things done. Even meditation comes to be commended as a form of relaxation or renewal, a refreshment, not for its own sake, but 'so that we can be more effective in our work' or 'to promote physical and mental well-being'. We treat it as though it were instrumental, a means to something else, instead of an end in itself.

It is no part of my task here to write at length about prayer. Bookshops these days are full of books on prayer, and there is no shortage of guides far more competent than I am. But it is probably necessary to underline this particular point in a book on the calling of God, namely that the primary calling to us is to be with God, to spend time in God's presence, not as a means to something else, but simply because God is and because we are made for relationship with God. That is the basic fact about prayer. I think it is Thomas Green who says somewhere that learning to pray is a matter of learning to waste time gracefully. How true that is! It is in the end totally useless and utterly important. It is what we are made for and is absolutely no use for anything else. That, it seems to me, is the spirit in which to approach it. It is that state of being, of idling or loitering, that allows us to be aware of an inner thirst, an inner longing for God which is just a fact of human existence, but which most of the time is covered over and hidden by layers and layers of activity and falsity; activity often just for the sake of it, because we feel vaguely guilty if we are not 'achieving something'. Many people never get down to prayer in any real sense of the word because they cannot cope with the apparent 'uselessness' of it.

However, all of us live in this action-oriented world. For most of us it takes quite a number of steps to see that there might even *be* a different mode of existence, apart from action, busyness, striving, achieving, and all the rest of it. Discovering this has certainly been a lengthy process for me. At theological college in the late fifties we were at least taught about prayer: but the impression I got was that it was all about grind and exertion. The then principal of the college, who used to lecture to us on prayer, used often to go for a walk after lunch. Sometimes he would take a student with him. He had a circular route along the roads of the surrounding countryside that was known as 'the grind'. It was all of a piece, what he lived and what he taught. But it was all about effort and was achieved by iron self-discipline.

Well, that is one approach to the life of the spirit. The trouble was that it chimed in too well with my own predisposition from my upbringing, which had thoroughly imbued me with the notion that Christianity was about striving and effort. Even that might have been all right if it had fitted my actual temperament – as distinct from my superimposed temperament. But it did not, and it took me many, many years to discover that it did not. During my initial years in parish work I struggled as best I could with the business of prayer, trying to put into practice what we had been taught. But it had never really taken any root in me. Looking back, I can see that it never connected in any real sense with who I am. Gradually my personal prayer life got whittled away. After about seven or eight years I decided to chuck the whole thing overboard. I gave up any kind of private prayer, and decided I would rely solely on the daily offices of morning and evening prayer for my devotional life. I half-expected some sort of divine punishment for this impiety. How could I be a priest and not pray? Nor did I have any kind of spiritual guide at the time. I used to make an annual retreat, but on the odd occasions when I had asked for personal spiritual guidance I had not felt I encountered much understanding. So, wondering where to turn, I pulled down from my partially inherited library, the works of St Teresa of Avila. I do not remember why I chose that: I think I was just grasping at any straw. In the following months, a few pages at a time, I read all her writings. I do not suppose I understood much of what she was on about in her descriptions of the higher reaches of prayer. I certainly did not aspire to them myself. But I did discover a very attractive human being, a courageous and determined lady, full of insight and honesty, and some of her perceptive comments, especially from her autobiography, rang bells with my own experience. In the matter of prayer, one sentence from *Way of Perfection* struck a particular chord in me: 'The soul is like an infant still at its mother's breast: such is the mother's care for it that she gives it its milk without its having to ask for it so much as by moving its lips' (*Complete Works of St Teresa*, tr. E. Allison Peers, Sheed & Ward 1946, p. 130). I began dimly to realize that that might be true, and to rest in it. It was no great flash of enlightenment, just a very faint lessening of the darkness, the beginnings of a perception that took another ten or fifteen years to sink in. And looking back I can see that some personal counselling I received during those years was an important factor in enabling it to do so.

This will not be the only time I shall need to enter a caveat about attaching too much weight to my experience. I quote it here merely to illustrate the importance – and the difficulty – of finding *your own* personal relationship with God. In no sense am I suggesting, 'This is the way; walk in it.' Heaven forbid! I certainly hope you will not have such a lonely and unsupported search. Remember, that was in the sixties, when action in the world was everything, and a sword, as it were, hung over the inner life and its importance. Nowadays there are many more resources for the inner search.

First, there is a spate of books by modern writers on prayer, as well as the spiritual classics. Anthony Bloom, Ruth Burrows, Charles Elliott, Richard Foster, Thomas Green, Joyce Huggett, Gerard W. Hughes, John Main, Anthony de Mello, and Thomas Merton spring to mind as modern and very readable exponents of a variety of different paths in spirituality.

Secondly, it is important, as far as it is possible, to sample different approaches, and not just to read about them. I personally believe that we learn far more by what we do than by what we are told. These days there are all kinds of prayer-groups, retreats, and prayer experiences on offer. One useful compendium that brings together quite a lot of these from across the ecumenical spectrum is *Retreats*, published annually by the National Retreat Association, The Central Hall, 256 Bermondsey Street, London SE1 3UJ.

Thirdly, it helps in your search for your way of encountering and relating to the living God if the approaches you try bear at least some relation to the type of person you are. Many people never really make any progress because the methods they try or are offered simply do not fit their temperament. There is much more awareness today of differences in temperament. Isabel Myers and her mother, Katharine Briggs, did a great deal of work on this in the decades following the publication in 1923 of C. G. Jung's seminal book *Psychological Types*. They evolved a method of identifying personality types and differences called the Myers-Briggs Type Indicator (outlined in *Gifts Differing* by Isabel Briggs Myers, Palo Alto, CA, Consulting Psychologists Press Inc. 1980), which in recent years has come to be used very widely. What I like about it is that it is affirmative. Unlike so many typologies, it helps you to identify your strong points, rather than pointing out your pathology. Most human qualities and characteristics are ambivalent, as the old declension has it – 'I am firm, you are stubborn, he is pig-headed.' Christians especially are often better at belabouring themselves for their weaknesses rather than affirming and exercising their good points. The Myers-Briggs approach helps you to be affirmative about what you are, rather than blaming yourself for what you are not. That is then a good starting point for exploring in the course of time the less developed sides of your nature. You will find Myers-Briggs work-shops advertised in *Retreats*, and some of these also focus on the implications of your temperament for the way you pray and seek to grow closer to God.

Fourthly, having a spiritual guide or companion, what Kathleen Fischer (*Women at the Well*, SPCK 1988) calls a spiritual midwife, is a great help. In fact a wise, loving and experienced spiritual guide is like gold – who can find her or him? But they do exist, often very much background people, who do not advertise themselves or have a compulsive need to help others, good listeners who also have first-hand experience of the joys and difficulties of their own search for God, people who are far enough on not to be hooked on -isms and fads, who have grown beyond the tradition which nurtured them and can see beyond the way they themselves follow, so that they can be genuinely open to another's spiritual journey. Just such a one is Anne Long, whose Grove booklet *Approaches To Spiritual Direction* is an excellent introduction to this whole field. For a fuller treatment of the pros and cons of *group* spiritual direction, have a look at chapter 7 of *Spiritual Friend* by Tilden Edwards (New York, Paulist Press 1980).

While we are on the subject of spiritual direction, it might be worth pointing out that it is not the same as counselling. Similar qualities are required in the guide or 'director', namely non-possessive warmth, personal genuineness and the capacity to listen. But the focus is different. The *basic* focus of counselling and psychotherapy is on the here and now of the relationship between client and counsellor. In spiritual direction the *basic* focus is on the relationship between the 'directee' and God. The two are not mutually exclusive of course; but a little clarity about the difference can help in sorting out the expectations of the directee (and also perhaps the director), the content of the sessions, the frequency of meeting, and so on.

What is important in the long run is that you discover *your* way in prayer. Trying other people's methods will help. They can be the vehicle for discovering God for yourself. But in the end there will be something unique in your relationship with God, something that has grown and come to be out of the quirks and quiddities of your own character and life history. Out of this evolves your personal response to the loving invitation to be with God, which will in the end extend far beyond any kind of formal times of prayer.

For a few people, the personal calling of God is simply to this contemplative dimension of life, a call to being rather than doing. Their calling is to witness by what they are and by their style of life to this dimension of existence in God. Maybe God calls some exclusively to this because its importance as one aspect of life for all of us is so little realized in our activist world. Be that as it may, the possibility of this kind of non-active personal calling does need to be borne in mind in what follows. But most of us are called to respond in active ways as well. We turn our attention now to that second aspect of God's double invitation.

3

A double invitation: 2

A would-be ordinand wrote: 'I want a job where I could *be* the job, instead of merely doing it.' That articulates very well the longing to be more wholehearted, more connected with what you are doing, more able to give yourself totally in what you do, a person to be rather than a job to do. But no job exists that will exactly fit all that you have it in you to be. The notion that a ready-made job of that kind is out there waiting for you is, in the end, a fantasy.

To be more wholehearted, more connected with what you do, requires much inner work. It is a symptom of the very extraverted nature of our society that we usually do not recognize this. We somehow expect it to happen from the outside, as it were. We search for a job out there; 'gi's a job', 'ordain me', or whatever. Whereas the real issue is an inner one: who am I and at this juncture what is the initiative that God wants to draw from who I am? Think of God's personal call to you as an invitation to sing your song, in John Powell's metaphor. But we live in a 'karaoke' society, if you see what I mean. Many people feel they have to dance to someone else's tune, to sing someone else's song. There is nothing wrong with that, up to a point. But it is a disaster if the whole of your life is lived like that. For God invites you to sing *your* song for others, *your* words, *your* music. And no one else can sing your song. In other words the inner sense of call is always to something that will be drawn out from within you, not something provided for you out there. It is always a call to take the risk of enacting your true self in some way for the enrichment of others.

It may well be that a job change could be for you a step in that direction, by being less ill-fitting or by giving you more self-determination. Through it you may discover a little more of who you are: after all, the exploration of your identity needs to be done in action just as much as in introspection or reflection. But God's personal call to you will always be beyond what is provided by any job specification, to an initiative unbidden by others, whether it is an aspect of your job or whether it means giving up your job. In the end God calls you to offer your very self in initiatives that require you to step out on unmarked paths.

That has certainly been my own experience. I was a parish clergyman for twenty-one years, and it was a privilege to work with the same congregation in some depth for fifteen of those years. But, as I said in the first chapter, there were aspects of the work that I found a real grind, especially in the early years. It was in the adult educational aspects of it that I first began to discover a sense of personal calling from God. As I responded to that in the parish context, God began, after a time, to nudge me further, in the direction of helping people beyond the bounds of my parish to link prayer and action in their lives. Latterly I began to look for a way of expanding the opportunities for that kind of ministry. Over a two-year period I applied for a variety of jobs which looked as if they might offer that – and was turned down for all of them. It was very painful at the time. Each rejection pushed me a little further down and each time it took me a little longer to pick myself up.

I am now so thankful that I failed to get any of those jobs. It meant I was forced to listen more carefully for God's personal leading, and in the end that meant resigning my parish and setting up a project from scratch, something I would never have dreamed of doing otherwise. I have told the story of this part of my life in more detail elsewhere (in my book *Live for a Change*). But I wanted at least to allude to it here, so that you can see that what I am talking about is based on my own experience as well as other people's.

God does not, of course, call everyone to throw away their livelihood like that. There are many, many other ways of setting out which feel every bit as demanding. For me personally at the moment, writing this book feels like that. Even though I was asked to write it, the request came from people who knew my general approach and that is why they asked me. I therefore have a free hand to do it any way I like. As it happens, it fits in with some ideas I already have. But the actual writing of it feels like rowing a boat single-handed across a trackless ocean. At times I have almost to tie myself to the chair to face this blank sheet of paper that stares up at me day after day and whispers, 'Come on, I want to hear what *you* have to say': and all the other sheets of paper I have already scribbled on that lie around me all over the place that mutter, 'This doesn't really express what you want to say – go on, try again.' And in my mind there is this chaotic jumble of thoughts and ideas that I have to try to wrestle into some sort of coherent order. You think I exaggerate? If I am not disciplined about it, *any* excuse will do to let myself off this hook. I think of a household errand to do, or I go and make a cup of coffee, or I need to get a bit of fresh air, or there's a letter or two that I simply must get into the post today.

That is one side of it: responding to a personal call of God always involves effort and struggle to offer who I really am, as opposed to second- or third-hand substitutes; and for me this includes warmed-over stuff that I have written myself in the past. The other side of it is, 'Woe is me if I do *not* write this book.' It is there inside me like a great undifferentiated lump to which I must somehow give expression, or perish inwardly in depression and meaninglessness. For better or worse at this moment in my life it is one of the things that I am born for. And though it is a struggle there is a profound longing to do it and at times a deep sense of satisfaction in doing it. Whenever we respond to God's personal call, whatever blood, sweat and toil is required, there is a deep joy about it. We know it is what we are for and we actually have a great time doing it.

It is always a risk quoting one's own experience. It can give much too narrow an impression of the kind of thing God calls people to. To help to guard against that, here are some words of Henry David Thoreau to take to heart:

> I would not have anyone adopt *my* mode of living on any account; for, beside that before he has fairly learned it I may have found out another for myself, I desire that there may be as many different persons in the world as possible; but I would have each one be very careful to find out and pursue *his own* way, and not his father's or his mother's or his neighbour's instead.
>
> (*Walden*, Penguin Classics 1986, p. 114)

And that goes for any other examples I shall give.

In the last two thousand years of church history, one of the traditional ways of responding to a personal call from God has been to become a monk or a nun. It is a way of self-dedication and of orienting oneself towards God. It is one way of living your response to 'I have called you by name and you are mine' (Isa. 43.1). There are some who say that one of the reasons why ordination candidates came to be quizzed about their personal sense of calling from the sixteenth century onwards was because of a confusion of the ordained ministry with the monastic life. Be that as it may, it is not unknown even for membership of a religious order to be just as much an other-determined role as many jobs in the secular world. Thomas Merton, who was himself a Cistercian monk, wrote, 'With us it is often . . . a case of men leaving the society of "the world" in order to fit themselves into another kind of society, that of the religious family which they enter. They exchange the values, concepts and rites of the one for those of the other' (*The Wisdom of the Desert*, Darley Anderson 1988, pp. 9–10). That is not to say that that is the case with all members of religious orders. Clearly it is not, but it is a danger, and one that Merton himself fell into in his early years as a monk. In his autobiographical *Elected Silence* (Hollis & Carter 1949, pp. 363–4) he wrote:

> By this time I should have been delivered of any problems about my true identity. I had already made my simple profession. And my vows should have divested me of the last shreds of any special identity. But then there was this shadow, this double, this writer who had followed me into the cloister . . . He is supposed to be dead but he stands and meets me in the doorway of all my prayers, and follows me into church . . . He generates books in the silence that ought to be sweet with the infinitely productive darkness of contemplation. And the worst of it is, he has my superiors on his side. Nobody seems to understand that one of us has got to die.

He was a young man in his thirties when he wrote that. It was a contradiction that dogged him for many years. But in the end it was the community monk that died, when at long last at his own request he was given permission to live as a hermit. His life, so well documented as it is in his own vast output of writing, is a very good illustration of a gradual process that is in one way or another one that we are all invited to live. It is a stage by stage process of responding to God's personal invitation to each of us. At first our response takes the form of ready-made roles or jobs or activities. For Merton this meant becoming a monk. Most of us need to have filled roles of one sort or another for quite a lot of years before we even *begin* to realize that there is more to us than will ever be defined by a role. It is that 'more' that is the focus of the inner sense of call. In the end God calls us out beyond any standardized role, even if the journey takes us through several such. For Merton it was in the end a call to a hermit life, which had up to that time not been permitted in his order: he had a great struggle to get the agreement of his superiors. For each of us it will always be something non-standard.

In case what I have just been saying may sound less than fair to religious communities, let me say this. I am not suggesting that becoming a monk or a nun necessarily prevents responsiveness to personal calling in its members, even if there is often a strong element of role-adoption at the novice stage. Perhaps it might be true to say that, at their best, religious communities are groups of people with a personal calling to ways of responding to God that are similar enough to enable them to join together in a common enterprise. But any institution or group does need to be *very* flexible in order to foster genuine openness to personal calling among its members.

Let me at this point quote at some length an example of what I am saying that may perhaps be nearer your own experience than a Cistercian monk is! Barry lives in the Midlands. Since he had done a degree in engineering, he felt obliged to go into engineering in industry for his first job. 'I was never gifted, certainly not on the practical side. I think I acted the role of an engineer. I did not enjoy the work. What stays in my mind from my years in industry are the people I met and worked with. I remember one senior manager who pointed out my lack of commitment as an engineer. I didn't appreciate the comment at the time. But looking back I'm very grateful to that man.' After four years of that he went into computing. 'Computing involved more numeracy than practical work, so initially it suited me. I worked more in a team, so this was good for my motivation. I moved from firm to firm to get promotion, first as a computing analyst, where I gained a knowledge of a particular computer system and felt a bit of a guru on it. I began to find myself in demand and of some value.' After a few years he moved on to be a junior manager in computers/engineering. But after two years he concluded: 'The management role was not me.'

His next move was to senior analyst in computing, in a team as part of a huge organization:

> I initially felt like a duck out of water. However, it was here that I began to feel I was doing something worthwhile. I was in a store in a manufacturing company, working with men on the shop floor and trying

36

to teach and encourage them to use a new computer system. This was a role of a different kind, but this time I was not 'acting'. These men were all that were left from a savage workforce-cutting scheme implemented by an authoritarian management. Some of the management regarded shop floor people as morons. Initially the storemen regarded me as one of the management – which I wasn't. Eventually they accepted me for who I was and I found myself becoming an encourager, teacher and to an extent sympathizer with their lot under some oppression.

I mention this because it seems to be a signpost for me, and one that was strongly in my mind during the exercises (from the book *Live for a Change*) we did at a diocesan weekend in April 1988. Other people's comments about me in the gift-naming exercise were things like: 'communication with young people – leadership skills – leads by example – inspires confidence – an enabler – encourages others, especially the underdog.' This was quite a surprise to me! My bosses at work saw me very differently. Early in 1988 they had commented on my lack of leadership, my lack of control of projects and people, my lack of aggression and drive.

My restlessness increased. Whilst on a computer course in London I felt at one point like smashing the computer. I looked out of the window at the traffic. On one lorry the carrier's name was B. Patient! Six months later it had got to the point where I knew I had to change what I was doing. I gave in my notice, not knowing what I would do, only that I must find something more worthwhile. The rector at our church had given a sermon where Jesus was asking Peter, 'Do you love me more than these – your nets, your livelihood?' God seemed to be saying something similar to me about computers, my livelihood. My wife was working, so we would manage financially. The rector also gave me some advice when I asked him how I was to discern God's will for me in what type of work I should do. He mentioned that the use of what gifts I have is very important.

I tried working with various disadvantaged groups, the mentally ill, mentally handicapped, elderly, and visually handicapped. Within the space of two weeks I had talked to or worked with a probation officer, social workers, care assistants, special needs teachers, vicar, friends, and employment training officers. I felt the most comfortable working as a volunteer at a college for the young visually handicapped where patience and teaching skills were needed. After a couple of months they offered me a job!

I never thought I would be working with young people. They were the one group of people I had tended to shy away from in the past. There were a number of people and events who pointed me in this direction. One was a chap at that diocesan weekend who thought I would be good working with young people (I thought he was mistaken at the time). Then there were a series of tiny incidents around that time that somehow made me aware of young people. For example I met a couple of aggressive teenagers in a citizens' advice bureau: I felt I could relate to them and understand their problems. To my surprise I wasn't afraid of them. On another occasion I happened on a teenage lad who had had a bad fall off his bike and gave him some help. Another time I was helping with a flag day collection and was reflecting that no young person had given anything, when seconds later a young chap comes up and does just that! Besides incidents like this there were many times when Scripture moved me and encouraged me in this direction.

There is something typical about all that. When you begin to be nearer to what God is on with in your life, when you begin to respond in action, even if it is only fumblingly, things have a way of happening like that. It is as though the Lord confirms the direction you are beginning to take with signs following. It does not take away your responsibility for your actions, but it often seems as though God comes more than half way to meet you.

Barry's story illustrates the sort of way a person begins to discover who they are in action. Only by filling other-determined roles for some years can you discover that there is more to you than that. No doubt in a few years Barry will discover there is more to him than his job working with the young visually handicapped, and will again become aware of the promptings of God to move on. Barry's story well illustrates how gradual the process usually is of coming to the point where it might be said that a person is responding to a personal call from God in a clear and explicit way. Barry has perhaps hardly got to that point even now. What seems to happen is that throughout our life God is always calling each of us to respond to him in a personal way, to give more and more what we are and could be. At first we may not be conscious of this at all. As young adults we are pretty much pulled around by circumstances, like Barry was. At this stage it could hardly be said that we are conscious at all of our own gifts and distinctiveness, or of God calling us in any explicit or practical sense. Only very, very gradually, perhaps through quite a number of job changes, do we become more self-aware and more aware of the deeper prompting of God.

Now of course throughout this process it is appropriate to speak of God calling us personally. However, usually when I use the phrase 'the personal calling of God' in these pages I mean it in the conscious developed sense, in the sense of an idiosyncratic initiative which a person takes with an explicit awareness of being called to it by God, which has also some confirmation from others. In other words I use the phrase to refer to the developed, explicit phases of what is actually an emerging process. This may seem too restricted a use of it, especially in view of the fact that most people, for all sorts of reasons, personal, political, and economic, are not at this stage. But consider a parallel from nature. It is no doubt possible to distinguish garden flowers by their stems, or even by their roots, for all I know. However, they are usually known by their flowers. In the same way I believe that we see God's personal calling of people most clearly in their flowering. God's call to all of us is to blossom and to bear fruit.

'Would that all the Lord's people were prophets' (Num. 11.29). Would that all Christians were responding to God's personal call to them. I want to depict as vividly as I can the flowering and fruit-bearing to which God calls us singly and together: because I long for people to flourish, for a mutual sharing of giftedness which would so transform our hurting souls and our troubled and divided world. I realize this is the longing for nothing less than the coming of the Kingdom here on earth as it is in heaven. You will tell me it is impossible this side of the grave: but that in no way dims the desire for it. And I believe this longing for God and this desire for God's Kingdom is present in all of us, though usually hidden away and covered over by more superficial desires.

To try to evoke more fully what I mean by this flowering, I want to quote again from Thomas Merton, a passage which beautifully expresses the personal calling of God to each human being. In his book *Conjectures of a Guilty Bystander* (Sheldon Press 1977, pp. 128–9) he describes a summer dawn in the valley where his monastery is set. When they rise for the night office at 2.15 a.m. there is no sound except in the abbey. By 3 a.m. there are the first stirrings in the valley:

> The first chirps of the waking day birds mark the '*point vierge*' of the dawn under a sky as yet without real light, a moment of awe and inexpressible innocence, when the Father in perfect silence opens their eyes. They begin to speak to him, not with fluent song, but with an awakening question that is their dawn state, their state at the '*point vierge*'. Their condition asks if it is time for them to 'be'. He answers 'yes'. Then, they one by one wake up, and become birds. They manifest themselves as birds, beginning to sing. Presently, they will be fully themselves, and will even fly . . . All wisdom seeks to collect and manifest itself at that blind sweet point . . . the virgin point between darkness and light, between non-being and being.

This is the universal call of God to every human being. The

secret, silent voice of God calling you into being, inviting you to offer your song, your part in the hymn of creation. I wonder what that virgin point that Merton speaks of means to you personally, that hesitantly and tremulously creative point between darkness and light, between the safety of the hiddenness within and the struggle to bring to birth into the light of day. Are you ever aware of that in your own life? Maybe sometimes you are aware of it in the brief twinkling it takes to decide whether to be honest or not at a particular moment in a conversation that seems to call for it or whether you take refuge in silence or in platitudes. Maybe sometimes you notice it in suddenly being aware, as you go about your daily activities, of a small kindness you could do or a contribution you could make: and you refrain, from the fear that you will make yourself vulnerable, 'I'll look foolish', or 'My offer may be rejected', or, 'So-and-so will undoubtedly misinterpret it'. Perhaps you have noticed it on a larger scale, in the beginnings of a desire to take some creative step, which you have acted on with a strong sense of inner rightness and peace: or which you have funked with the subsequent depressed feeling of having been basically untrue to yourself?

These are the kinds of ways you begin to be aware of God's personal calling; not usually in the grand gesture, but in these tiny daily opportunities to be truer to what you are and could be. As you begin to live a little more in this kind of way God will begin to call you to take more distinct and perhaps more noticeable initiatives, which then begin to be more identifiable to yourself and others as a calling from God. But writ large or writ small, the process is fundamentally the same. 'The longest journey starts with but a single step.' And however long the journey is, and however publicly visible it may be, subjectively it feels like just a step at a time.

Hugh Prather said of his book *Notes to Myself* (Lafayette, Real People Press 1970):

> After I had written this book I told several friends. Their response was polite and mild. Later I was able to tell them the book was going to be published. Almost to a man they used the words, 'I am proud of you.' Proud of the results but not of the action. Everyone but me looks back on my behaviour in judgment. They can only see my acts coupled with their results. But I act now and I cannot know the results.

Exactly: and this factor does make it quite difficult to speak about the personal calling of God. Our response to God's personal calling

is *always* in the moment, from moment to moment. The attempt to
describe it is liable to falsify it by appearing to give it much too solid
or permanent a quality; because when one describes it it is usually
past. For example when you read what I am writing now it will be in
black and white on a printed page. But as I write it, I do so haltingly,
a phrase or sentence at a time on the trackless void of the paper in
front of me. The feel of this to me is *totally* different from what it
looks like to you. And so it is usually with responding to the personal
calling of God.

Nevertheless, with full awareness of the risks of misinterpretation,
but having done my best to draw attention to them, I want now to
describe some activities of a number of people that seem to me to
have the flavour of a developed response to the personal calling of
God. The main reason why I do this is to encourage you to open
your mind to the possibilities in your own life, which are always
much wider than we imagine them to be.

One of the features of personal calling is that usually God calls us
to unearth and to offer our giftedness in relation to some aspect of
the world's pain. Jim Hennequin is a clear example (*Observer
Magazine*, 11 March 1990). In collaboration with *Spitting Image* he and
others are developing the use of man-made air-muscles such as are
used in the *Spitting Image* puppets, to create a robot arm for the use of
disabled people. 'I think the process of good professional invention is
opening your mind to the problem' – in this case human disabilities
on the one hand, and on the other a possible air-controlled aid. His
God-given gift is the capacity to see and create solutions that other
people seem not to be able to see. He is obviously a non-conforming
character who sees all sorts of possibilities that the rest of us are too
dim to see and too standardized in our expectations even to imagine.
That to me is a faithful mirror of one facet of God's nature. One of
the features of God's way of doing things that shines out from the
pages of the Bible is that it is always unexpected, always non-
standard. God has always seen possibilities for hope, for justice, for
help, for healing, or for human flourishing that no one else has. The
prophets were cast in the same mould. This is what *we* are to do, to
open our minds and hearts to some aspect of the world's need, and
to open our imagination and our spirit to God's prompting.

There is a great need for lateral thinking in opening ourselves to
God's call. Most of us need some healing in the area of our tunnel

vision, our sheer smallness of mind. Even if we do begin to open our tiny minds, the words that too easily rise to our lips are, 'It's impossible to do anything about that. That's just the way things are. You can't change that.' Richard is one who is not put off by such thoughts. He is the regional agent for a major British bank. He is its eyes and ears for the economic performance of his region. He is in regular touch with some hundreds of companies of all types and sizes, and monitors their financial health, the impact of policy changes, and so on. One of his hopes is to see the regions compete more effectively with London, for the long-term health of both London and the regions. For several years he has worked to promote his city as an independent financial centre. 'We in this region can meet most of the needs of most of the companies most of the time.' Some years ago he founded a regional financial forum to help to achieve this. At first it was the big firms that joined: but once they had dived in and made themselves at home, they were reluctant to admit the tiddlers. But Richard, with deeply held objections to élitism, felt, 'If anyone wants to shout for this city we should welcome them!' But he had, as he put it, 'the heck of a battle to persuade the other members'.

Within his own company he longs for it to be 'a worthy employer of people', and it has become less so in recent years. 'The human dimension has been more and more subordinated to budgetary control. There is far too much emphasis on technical ability. We need technically able people, but who are also well-rounded managers.' Richard himself left school at seventeen with only O-levels and feels he has been very fortunate to get where he has. He personally tries to make sure that the bank does not close its doors to people who do not have high educational attainments. He instanced a young woman in the bank's employ. He is sure she has managerial potential. 'In this particular field this requires the capacity to master and to filter a mass of information and take decisions based on that. It is very difficult to give junior employees experience of this, and this woman will never get anywhere without it. The bank would normally move her to London for six months to give her a try in its head office. But she has a young family and a difficult domestic situation and six months away in London would be a virtual impossibility.' So, in order for her to get this kind of experience, Richard had arranged for her to be seconded to a commercial bank in his own city. This is unheard of. Persuading a local bank was the first hurdle, because there was absolutely nothing in it for them. Then he had to try and persuade his head office to agree. To cap it all, the woman herself met the whole idea with total disbelief, 'You've got to be joking!' That is often the price of taking creative initiatives.

Opening yourself to hear God's personal call also requires openness to the world's pain; and that means listening to people and to situations with an open mind, rather than barging in with ready-made answers which more often than not reflect our own prejudices about 'what these people need'. Susan lives in a large industrial town in the north of England. One Sunday morning in his notices the vicar spoke of a need for church people to be able to learn about their faith in terms of their own life experiences, and he said that a parish working party was hoping to get something going along these lines. Susan was a member of this working party. After the service, Ann came up to Susan and said, 'I come to church on my own without my husband and it's really quite difficult at times. I would appreciate being able to meet with some other women in the same position as me, just to talk about it and get a bit of support. Is that the sort of thing that you are going to do?' Well, Susan had not thought of that. But when she began to think, she realized there were quite a number of women in the congregation in that position. The first thing she did was to meet with Ann to hear about how she saw it. Ann described how difficult churchgoing was for her, since her husband and family were so anti-church. It was often all right to come on a Sunday; but anything beyond that could cause a great deal of friction at home. As they talked Susan began to realize how little she knew of what Ann had to cope with. She remembered times when other churchgoers had been very critical of Ann, 'Why doesn't she come every Sunday morning?' 'Why doesn't she pull her weight on the stewardship committee?' Susan was beginning to understand why. To cut a long story short, a group of women convened by Susan and Ann has now met on a number of occasions on a weekday morning (when the menfolk are out at work, to avoid unnecessary aggravation) and they have found it extremely helpful – a no-holds-barred sharing of women's experience in a working-class community and an exploration of what it means to be a Christian in those circumstances.

Ezekiel wrote, 'I came to the exiles at Telabib who dwelt by the river Chebar and I sat where they sat, overwhelmed for seven days' (3.15). One of Susan's gifts is the capacity to listen and put herself in someone else's shoes. To some extent this is a matter of discipline and can be learnt. It is a prerequisite for being open to God's calling and is something we should constantly cultivate.

One of the reasons why we do not 'hear' other people's pain is because we have blanked off our own pain. This is not usually deliberate. It is a kind of natural safety curtain which helps to safeguard our own personal emotional equilibrium. But it has a way of making us impervious to other people's pain as well. The reason for this is that allowing ourselves to feel for others has a way of reactivating our own dormant inner wounds. The safety curtain protects our peace of mind, especially if the latter is a little precarious. But peace of mind of this kind is a luxury to be forgone by those who would open themselves to God's calling. That process will always bring us pain and distress as an integral part of it. And if we carry some unhealed wounds within us, as all of us do in some measure, they may well be reactivated. Most of us need to be listened to ourselves at times so that we can discharge pent-up fears and anger, griefs and hurts, which otherwise form a hard shell of scar tissue, unfeeling and inflexible. I would say that everyone who would open themselves to God's personal calling will need counselling for themselves. In fact there is frequently a close connection between your own pain and what God calls you to do.

That has been true of me. God's calling of me to work with others on the issue of personal calling arose from my own sometimes painful experience as a parish priest. I never wanted to be ordained. My father was a priest and I knew too much of what it might involve. The only reason I offered myself was because people would keep asking me if I was going to follow in my father's footsteps. I hoped that if I went to a CACTM (as it was then) selection conference they would turn me down and that would settle it once for all. They did not.

That was more than forty years ago. But my (sometimes pain-filled) struggle to fill that role caused me to reflect much on the many aspects of the calling of God. In the end God brought me to the point where it was clear that I should resign from my parish in order to be faithful to the gradually maturing sense of God's personal calling to work with others on this issue in a more freelance way.

That is in no way to say that I regret being ordained or that it was the wrong decision or anything like that. In any case I could not have resigned and launched out one single day earlier than I actually did at the end of 1981. For one thing I would have been too frightened; I would not have had enough confidence to ask for the necessary support from others; and quite simply it would never have occurred to me to set out, Abraham-like, in that kind of way. As it was, the idea was only born of the sheer and utter desperation of being unable to find any other means of moving forward: and it was actually someone else, a dear friend, who helped me to crystallize the possibility.

Let me give one or two other examples of people for whom a willingness to face and carry their own pain in one way or another has been a factor in the kind of activity or offering to which God has called them. Patsy was someone who, as she grew to adulthood, had a great deal of inner pain to cope with. Like most of us, she was very ambivalent about how much she wanted to face it. Then, to cap it all, her beloved brother died as a result of AIDS. In a kind of a way that has become a blessing. It was at least a death that led to a resurrection for her. It brought her to seek some fairly thorough-going counselling for herself, and eventually led to her setting up a counselling and befriending service for people diagnosed as HIV positive and their families, with a strong sense that this is God's calling to her at the moment.

In the case of Di, the connection with her own pain was less direct, easier to see in retrospect. Many years ago she had a rather unusual job as a home/school liaison teacher. She had no children of her own. In fact she suffered ill health which made it impossible for her to have children. But her work brought her into contact with mothers and young children all the time. Sometimes in a nursery she would notice the look on the faces of some of the mothers; of utter exhaustion when they could just sit down and let someone else cope with their children for a while; of relief when a young mother instead of always having to do the caring could actually be listened to herself for once. To cut a long story short, when they had moved to another part of the country, Di started an organization called PATCH in her home town. That is an acronym for Parent And Toddler Care at

Home; they train and organize volunteers to provide for some of these needs in their own communities. It was set up with a great deal of careful groundwork and liaison with people in the field of local education and health.

Years later Di was able to have children herself; and she joined a PATCH group. She would go along and others would take responsibility for her children for a while. And she would just flop in a chair. 'Sometimes I would sit and talk to people, and sometimes just collapse in a heap and sit there in a stupor. Occasionally I'd have a cry. But I would always come away feeling refreshed.' Di had been childless and had suffered the heartache of being unable to have children. Looking back she is surprised she was so aware of the needs of young mothers at that time. But she does feel that in a way PATCH was her child in the years before she had children of her own.

Pain, your own and others', is a factor in the development and discernment of personal calling. But so is pleasure and play. Ten years ago Mary came to a fairly large one-day workshop on the Exodus theme, run in a local college hall. 'I was still at the bottom of a deep trough of post-retirement and bereavement. The question was asked, "If you could be or do anything you liked in your wildest dreams, what kind of future would you invent for yourself?" No strings, just complete freedom of choice – what? The question seemed unanswerable: "Don't know" was the dismal reply – thought, if not spoken. My sense of inner and outer bleakness remained. But it was a teasing question that would not go away.'

From childhood Mary had loved flowers and the out-of-doors. 'My grandfather was a gardener; I would have dearly loved to have been a gardener. But it was not for girls in my day.' She earned her living as a librarian, but she remembers the magic and enthusiasm communicated in a WEA class on botany. The lecturer was the then unknown David Bellamy. Through him she has for the last thirty years been involved in a local conservation trust, which gave her a chance to indulge her delight in the living world. A few weeks after that Exodus workshop she was browsing through a conservation journal and noticed an advertisement for a tour to the Seychelles led by David Bellamy. '*That's* what I would like to do! Could that be the answer to the teasing question? Surely not? Wouldn't it have to be something with an element of being useful to people, VSO or something like that? Surely it couldn't be something just for my own enjoyment? Anyway, where was I going to find the money?' An unexpected legacy from a relative solved that, and eighteen months later, 'I was on my way to what General Gordon called "the original Garden of Eden".'

That became for her not just 'a stepping stone out of the trough, but a springboard to a new life of action, interest, friends and enjoyment'. It led first to her enrolling in an Environment Management course run by the Adult Education department of a nearby university; this was after much hesitation, which was not helped by friends: 'What do you want to go studying for at your age?' Since then she has become involved 'in politics, of all the most unlikely things. I became a Green, even standing in a local council election.' In the past year she has organized a local environmental awareness day, and been involved in the preparation of the Church's participation in the National Garden Festival at Gateshead. 'That's quite a challenge, for up to now the churches have not seemed to be in the forefront in environment issues.' So play, enjoyment, pleasure, doing what in your heart of hearts you love to do is another central strand in the discernment of personal calling.

So is free-wheeling and allowing yourself space to dream dreams. Stephen's dream came to him in the bath. He was brought up a Congregationalist in West Yorkshire. His family loved the Lake District and on their visits there used to worship at Carver Congregational church in Windermere. The church is set in beautiful grounds, and at one end of the gardens is what was then the manse. As a young adult, having worked for three years in a bank, he was accepted for training as a minister:

> Not long into the first year I asked the Principal, 'How many colleges have we for training parsons?' 'Nine,' he said. 'How many colleges do we have to train the rest of the church?' 'None,' was the slightly puzzled reply. 'Aren't there more of them than us?' I asked. Shortly afterwards, having a bath, I had a dream of that old manse at Windermere turned into a training centre for the whole Church, to equip it for life and witness in the world; and the local church at Windermere revitalized, and putting on music and drama for the summer visitors.

He talked about it to a friend, who is now Moderator of one of the provinces of the United Reformed Church, and wrote it down and sent it to the then Moderator of the Lancashire Union of the

Congregational Church, to which Windermere belonged, 'thinking that someone far brighter than me would bring it to fruition'. That was in 1960. Many times in the early years of his ministry Stephen visited Carver with the groups of young people from his church he used to take walking in the Lakeland hills. Each time he hoped to see some signs of activity, but there seemed to be none.

When you have been given a little glimpse of a tiny corner of God's dream for the world, and you begin to wish someone would do something about it, sooner or later God has a way of putting the question back to you, 'What are *you* going to do about it?' That has been my experience; and it was Stephen's, too. 'Every quarter we ministers get a list of vacant pastorates; and just when it was right for us to be leaving Upton-by-Chester, my second pastorate, there was Windermere on the list,' since 1972, of course, part of the United Reformed Church, as he himself is now. He made enquiries to see if anything of his hopes for a training centre had materialized. There was nothing. 'Maybe in 1960 that might have been possible,' said the Moderator over the phone, 'but not now.' The local church was weak, Stephen was told. There was no money, and no vision:

> By the urging of the Spirit, I remonstrated and said that if no one else was going to go, then I would, if it were possible. Amazingly, in January 1982, I was inducted to the pastorate at Windermere; though no one really believed that the church there would revive, or that there would be a training centre, except me – and God. I asked a member from Upton to sing 'Be not afraid' from Mendelssohn's *Elijah* at the Induction. I was petrified!

As well he might be, especially if he had known the forces that would be ranged against him. He had 'endless battles with those who said it was impossible, unnecessary, wouldn't work, could never happen, there wasn't the money, it was the wrong place, it would never make ends meet'. Take note of that, if you plan to be open to God's personal calling to you. It is the devil's litany: and you will hear it intoned by all sorts of good people. They can of course be right at times, and it does need careful discernment. But Stephen had done that, and what was now needed was perseverance. In 1986, after £350,000 worth of building and alteration, the centre began its work of 'enabling the Church to receive new life and equipping all God's people for work in his service'. Stephen himself then moved on to new work.

As the hopes begotten by your God-given dream begin to become incarnate in action that is often the place where you begin to encounter the cross. That is what Robert found. He is a parish priest whose hobby is calligraphy, 'not the prettily-lettered cards you find in craft shops next to the soft toys. I think that's a barrier to people recognizing that for some this is a means of genuinely artistic expression.' He has loved art, and especially lettering, ever since he was a child, though he remembers a lot of discouragement from his perfectionist father. But that never killed his enjoyment of the physical act of writing. 'The work I really enjoy is purely alphabetical. It's the colours and the shapes, rather than the words.' Latterly, as he has become more expert, he likes to use some of the traditional tools, 'to pick up a quill pen and write on vellum makes it even more pleasurable'. He now does some part-time chaplaincy to the arts, and amongst other things has become acquainted with both amateur and professional calligraphers. Some years ago he began to conceive the idea of re-creating a monastic scriptorium, to experience the feel of producing a book by the ancient methods. When he mentioned it to the sponsoring body of his chaplaincy, they were very scornful and dismissive, 'Who on earth would be interested in *that*?' To cut an involved story short, he eventually won them round and came, together with a professional calligrapher and a deacon with experience of leading retreats, both of whom he very much looked up to as experts in their field, to run a retreat for calligraphers on Lindisfarne. Twelve people enrolled, and formed four working groups, of one of which Robert himself was a member. Even though the idea of the retreat had come from him, he felt he should take a relatively back seat in the running of it.

They were not there to learn calligraphy. They were expert enough in that. Robert's intention was that they would produce something that would be of use to visitors in the chapel of the small conference house where they were staying. They would have to work together, both to generate the idea for the book or books, and to produce them as a co-operative effort, all within the framework of four daily services of psalms and readings; the whole informed by a kind of Benedictine understanding of work and worship as a means of encountering God.

If you have any knowledge or experience of the way people function in groups, you would guess that Robert was in for a hard time. Remember, these people were artists – not renowned for their capacity to work together. But the experienced and the knowledge-able usually know too much ever to get into trying to translate impossible dreams into reality. Often it is left to those of us who are naive and unaware of the difficulties. That often seems to be the way of it; perhaps God knows we are easier pushovers for the work of the Kingdom. I am not against knowledge and understanding – far from it. But it *can* prevent us taking the risks that are always involved in responding to the calling of God.

It is perhaps inappropriate to chronicle in detail the difficulties encountered in practice on this retreat, and the miseries suffered by Robert in those four days, and also I guess by some of the other members; except to say that at one point in despair he himself nearly pulled out. It brought him face to face with his own perfectionism, and also with his propensity to admire the qualities of others and to hide his own light safely under a bushel (Matt. 5.15) – a temptation to most of us to some degree. It also brought him a good deal of flak from some of the other members. But through it he discovered also within himself a God-given capacity to love, even the most difficult, opinionated and cripplingly unco-operative people.

As he looks back on it, he sees it as a battle, the kind of battle people like Cuthbert and other hermits withdrew to fight, an inner battle of which the hermit is at the very centre. This retreat had that sort of quality about it; it brought the members face to face with themselves and one another and with God within themselves and each other. I almost hesitate to add that in the course of the retreat they produced four beautiful and artistically harmonious little books around the theme of the seasons, a real feast for eyes and heart – lest it might be thought that that was the measure of the 'success' of the retreat.

Those then are some examples of the sorts of ways God calls people into being as agents of his Kingdom. I have chosen them to try to illustrate some of the distinctive features of personal calling. But all these examples are of people doing things. Let me add one more. At a recent weekend workshop on personal calling the members were describing their present perception of it in their own lives. The last person but one to speak was an elderly widow. She began by saying that she was more aware now of God inviting her to respond to his love. But he didn't seem to be calling her to any new activity; somehow she expected he would. I suggested that maybe God was calling her simply to be responsive to his love; perhaps that was her calling at present. She replied she thought she 'ought to have grown beyond that at her age'!

It is at times like that when I wonder if any human being can ever help another discover their calling from God! Whatever precautions you take it is *so* easy to create expectations which actually prevent people from hearing. I am reminded of one of Janet Morley's collects: 'O unfamiliar God, we seek You in the places You have already left and fail to see You even when You stand before us . . .' (*All Desires Known*, SPCK 1992, p. 14).

'The Stranger in the wings is waiting for his cue, the fuse is always laid to some annunciation,' wrote Louis MacNeice. The annunciation and the virgin birth are key passages for the understanding of personal calling. 'The Holy Spirit will come upon you and the power of the most high will overshadow you . . . you shall conceive and bear a son' (Luke 1.35, 31 NEB) are words addressed to every Christian, if only we are listening. Each of us has some task that is ours to do, some gift to give to the life of the world. This is your baby, the child you conceive through the fertilizing power of God. There may be many such children for you to bring to birth and to nurture in the course of your life. And like flesh and blood children, they are not your private possessions. They are God's gifts to the world through you. Mary, the mother of Jesus, exhibits the pattern of this process. It requires of us four things. First, it requires openness to God. By this I mean openness to the reality of God, the love and majesty and unexpectedness of God, the compassion and generosity and creativity of God. Mary was willing to listen to and receive the astonishing and totally unexpected message of the angel. Secondly, it requires obedience. By this I mean not obedience to some externally imposed law, but obedience to the deepest law of your own nature, given to you by God, and called forth to be a gift to others. 'Be it unto me according to your word,' according to your dawn call to me. Thirdly, it requires a willingness to set out at God's bidding, one step at a time, without knowing the outcome. Mary had absolutely no idea what would be required of her. She would only discover that as she took each step. That requires courage. Fourthly, it requires a readiness to meet the cross, as Mary did, to see our precious offering

51

spurned, or maimed, or rubbished, through the spite, or the envy, or just the incomprehension of others.

'Be it unto me according to your word' (Luke 1.38). God's word to Mary is a unique word addressed to her, a specific person in a specific situation, inviting her to undertake a specific task. So it is with each one of us. 'We are all Mary, virgin and undelivered, to whom the announcement has been made, in whom the infant grows' (M. C. Richards). One of her son's parables (Luke 8.5–15) also likens the word of God to a seed sown in our hearts, and describes how we fail to receive the seed or allow it to germinate. But, thank God, there are those who hearing God's word to them, hold it fast in an honest and good heart, and bring forth fruit with courage and perseverance.

It may be that some of my readers may be wondering about the place of sin in the way of looking at the Christian life that I am putting forward in these pages. I hope that it is already clear, but in case it is not, let me spell it out plainly. Sin is basically the failure to respond to God's invitation. Think of the parable of the sower as a parable of personal calling. Sin is when the seed falls on the footpath and is trampled, or when it falls on the rock and fails to take root. Sin is when it falls among thistles and we are seduced by the glamorous, or the superficial, or the safe; when we prefer to feed our egos or guard our imagined securities, rather than risk responding to God's personal word to us. Sin is the chains that bind us in myriad ways and prevent us taking wings at God's loving invitation. Some of these chains are self-chosen, the result of personal choices we each make: some are forged by the fact that our lives are inextricably bound up with a world that is not responsive to God.

I am not one of those who believe that human nature is irredeemably corrupt. I believe that within all of us, however deeply buried and however squashed or twisted, lies the capacity to be responsive to God. Jesus showed us what it means to be responsive. In his ministry he lived the love of God for the world and in doing so to the death exposed us and it for what we are, frightened, security-conscious, life-avoiding, and apt to enshrine these tendencies in our corporate institutions. As his sisters and brothers we too are called to be responsive, not as Jesus clones, but as ourselves. We are to catch the same vision and longing for the coming of the Kingdom as Jesus did, and to open ourselves to the same risks as he did. Mostly we are unresponsive, held back by fear, crippled by our wounds, bamboozled by superficial delights, chained by the institutions and value systems which we create and of which we are part. But God is with us in Jesus, sometimes to confront us, but always to love us into life and responsiveness.

You may be realizing that responding to God's personal calling to you could be a hard road. It could be hard to find what is your message, your song, your act of love. And it could require a lot of courage to put that into practice. It could mean following a lonely road, and one that would make you different from others. You are right. It is the narrow way and the narrow gate that Jesus speaks of (Matt. 7.14). But happy are those who find it; because it is the way to life both for you and through you for others. It will mean finding your uniqueness, and that does mean finding the courage to step out of the crowd. But it will bring you to a much more genuine closeness to others. It will not be the closeness of those who are too frightened to be different. It will be the companionship of the colours of the rainbow where each very different colour has its own unique part to play in the corporate spectrum of the Kingdom.

4

RSVP

'What must I do to attain holiness?' asked an earnest enquirer. 'Follow your heart,' said the preacher. 'Heresy!' cried a bystander. The bystander had been brought up on *The Book of Common Prayer*, which regarded following the devices and desires of your own heart as a definition of sin. He could be right. In these days when 'every man for himself' has been raised to the level of a political creed it might do us no harm to have a dose of BCP now and then, to remind us that following the devices and desires of our own hearts can lead us into ways that are very damaging and destructive to our fellow citizens.

But there is more to be said. Following your own heart means something a bit deeper than adding noughts to your annual income. It means following the longings and aspirations of your deeper and greater self. To begin to do that you must dig down, past your imagined wants or needs, past your desire for status or recognition. And that is not easy: because most of us are out of touch with our true selves, seduced by our more superficial wishes, driven, sometimes, by the fears and foibles of our inner child of the past.

When I was young holiness held no attractions for me whatever. There was a sort of bloodlessness about it; the face of holiness presented to me was a pallid and life-denying one. I knew that being a Christian was about doing the will of God. But to my young mind the will of God felt like alien and impossible demands made upon an unwilling heart. It was a matter of gritting your teeth, like walking twenty miles over the Yorkshire moors into a storm of wind and driving rain. And it definitely meant squashing all your natural inclinations. If you actually liked doing the will of God, then you had got it wrong – it couldn't possibly be what God wanted of you. Being a Christian meant crushing your own spirit and putting on Christ. And to my young shoulders that felt about as comfortable and about as light as a suit of medieval armour. Thank God, those notions are not so widespread today. But they are still around. They remind me of one of the Schulz cartoons. The Peanuts children are looking at the charred remains of Snoopy's kennel. Lucy: 'So your house burnt down! So what? A little tragedy now and then will make you a better person. Man was born to suffer.' Charlie Brown: 'He's not a man, he's a dog.' Lucy: 'The theology is the same.' Snoopy climbs up and lies on what is left of his kennel and mutters: 'I don't believe it! Dogs were born to bite people on the leg and to sleep in the sun!'

I don't believe it either. I agree with Snoopy's more affirmative theology. In the more recent decades of my life I have come to believe that basically the will of God goes *with* the grain of your being rather than across it. That is not to say that that will always be the case. It is rather to say that until you have discovered the truth of that in your own life, until you have encountered the with-the-grain-ness of God's will, you are likely to misinterpret the instances when it is across the grain as the dictates of a slave-driving God.

One of the mentors who brought me a gospel of grace rather than law was Elizabeth O'Connor, through her books. In *Eighth Day Of Creation* (Word Books 1971) she wrote: 'We ask to know the will of God, without guessing that his will is written into our very beings' (p. 15). What joy, if that were true – if being godly or holy might sometimes and in some sense go with the grain of my deepest longings and my innermost being. I have come to believe that basically it does. The problem for most of us is how to be enough in touch with our innermost selves to know what our deepest longings really are.

We must now turn our attention to this. How to be more in touch with your deeper self, how to discern God's personal call to you, how to be more responsive to God. I have offered an approach to this at much greater length in my *Live for a Change*. Here in this chapter is a much briefer outline in eight sections. At the end of each one there is something for you to do, because I believe you learn more by doing, and that your learning is more truly your own: and after all this is a matter which you need to explore for yourself.

You will need to take your time over this. What I suggest you do is to read through the whole book first, including this chapter, and then if you want to do some practical exploration of God's personal calling to you, as I hope you will, come back and do these exercises later, perhaps spread over several days or weeks. For them to be any help you will need unhurried time for reflection. In an age of instant answers and blared messages it is very difficult to adjust our pace to God's ways and attune our hearing to the quiet and unspectacular prompting of God. But without that adjustment, we shall remain deaf and impervious to God's personal invitations to us. It will also help if you are able to share with others your experience of doing these exercises. Any house-group whose members have a good level of personal honesty and a willingness to listen, and who can allow one another to be different, will be a big help.

I shall use as a framework some passages from the Exodus saga. That saga is in a way the prototype of calling and discipleship and it has both an individual and a corporate dimension. It is one of the main death and resurrection cycles in the Old Testament. You may ask why I am not using the life and death of Jesus as the model of personal calling here. There are three reasons. First, I have done so elsewhere (in my *Live for a Change*). Second, Jesus himself, according to Luke, saw in the Exodus saga the prototype of his own calling: at the transfiguration he talked with Moses and Elijah about the exodus he was to complete in Jerusalem (Luke 9.31). Third, I think that for some of us the Exodus saga is more accessible in the sense that it offers more immediate parallels to our own backsliding humanity: there is a temptation in some quarters to place Jesus' earthly ministry on too lofty a pedestal, which distances his humanity, and emphasizes the gulf between us and him rather than what we have in common with him.

I shall not be attempting an exposition of the Exodus passages. I shall simply be inviting you to find illumination and encouragement from them in your own journey of responsiveness to God. Nor is too much importance to be attached to the order of the sections. Each of the eight sections is designed to draw attention to one facet of what is a multi-faceted process. But it needs to be borne in mind that it is a life-long process we are dealing with, and we need to continue to grow in each of its aspects throughout our life. None of them is ever finished and done with, this side of the grave. As we respond, God always calls us on further.

I. YOUR PERSONAL HISTORY

Read Exodus 2.1–10 and reflect on it.

Begin to reflect on your own personal history. 'The Lord called me before I was born, he named me from my mother's womb' (Isa. 49.1). That is as true for each of us as it was for Moses (cf. Exodus 33.12). God has been calling you into being right from the moment of conception, through your months in your mother's womb, through the narrows of birth, through your time of physical and emotional dependence on your parents, through the turmoil of teenage, through the adventures of young adulthood, through the jobs and roles prescribed for you by society, to respond more and more as a mature, differentiated person and as a life-bringing member of the human community. Isaiah says, 'He named me from my mother's womb.' God's name for you is not the name by which you are known to other people. It is a unique name, known only to God, the new name, written on a white stone (Rev. 2.17), which symbolizes the developed, differentiated person you are invited to become through your responsiveness to the personal calling of God.

What God calls you to is always to some extent related to your gifts and to your disabilities, the ups and, more often, the downs of your life; frequently it takes its roots in your own healed wounds or shouldered suffering. But there is always an element of newness about it, even of radical newness and unexpectedness, revealing something of the endless inventiveness and resourcefulness of God against all expectations. If we are to be open to this leading most of us need some kind of counselling. All of us have times when we need to be listened to with unconditional acceptance and with appropriate space so that we can let go of the attachments and the fetters of the past. Pointing to another paradigm of calling, Martin Buber writes:

> God said to Abraham: 'Get thee out of thy country, and from thy kindred, and from thy father's house, unto the land that I will show thee.' God says to man: 'First, get you out of your country, that means the dimness you have inflicted on yourself. Then out of your birthplace, that means out of the dimness your mother inflicted on you. After that, out of the house of your father, that means out of the dimness your father inflicted on you. Only then will you be able to go to the land that I will show you.'
>
> (*Ten Rungs*, New York, Schocken Books 1947, p. 70)

Something to do. One of the first steps in this process is to write your spiritual history. I would suggest that you do not interpret the word spiritual too narrowly. Include all the experiences of whatever kind that have been significant for you, regardless of how unimportant or unspiritual they might seem to others. To help you, I list below some of the salient features of the Exodus saga. For the purpose of the present section of this chapter, reflect on their meaning and associations in connection with your own individual life, past and present. I have added some questions to help to get your reflection going. Write notes for yourself, or draw doodles, in response to each:

EGYPT   What have been, or are, the Egypt experiences of your life?

What are or have been for you places or times of being oppressed or ground down?

What roles or tasks that are demanded or expected of you feel like a kind of slavery?

Consider your character and inner life; which aspects of your own nature are disenfranchised, without voice or expression?

Which parts of you are imprisoned or squashed?

PHARAOH   What tyrants or oppressors are there in your life? e.g. the tyranny of unquestioned assumptions, your own or others?

What inner – or outer – Pharaohs are you personally aware of?

In what ways do you oppress or bully yourself? Or others?

MOSES   What frail or vulnerable new beginnings are there in your life?

What has been your experience of taking initiatives?

BURNING   As you look back over your life what particular
BUSH   experiences of God have made an impression on you, however insignificant or improbable they might sound to others?

In what circumstances do you tend to be spontaneously aware of God?

Is there some way you could more deliberately open yourself to God, or increase your awareness of God?

RED SEA   What steps could you take, or have you taken in the past, out of your personal Egypts?

What are or have been your feelings about the crossing?

What help do you need to make the crossing now?

DESERT   What are or have been desert experiences for you?

How have you felt about them?

What, for you, is water from the rock, or manna, or quails?

PROMISED   If you could be or do anything you liked in your
LAND   wildest dreams, what kind of future would you invent for yourself? What would you love to do?

PEOPLE IN   Who do you most identify with, or have most fellow
THE SAGA   feeling with – e.g. Pharaoh, Pharaoh's daughter, the Hebrew midwives, Moses, Aaron, Israelites, Egyptians, Jethro, Zipporah, Miriam, Caleb, the spies in Numbers 13, etc?

Look back over what you have written or drawn.
What might God be saying to you in all this?

2. MAKE SPACE FOR SILENCE AND FREEWHEELING

Read Exodus 2.15b–22 and reflect on it.

I take this aspect at this stage, not because it particularly belongs here; but because, since it is important at every stage if we are to be open to God's calling, I want to introduce it early on. Moses was evidently the good-hearted activist, who saw the appalling conditions besetting his fellow countrymen, and simply felt he could not stand by and do nothing. But he muscled in without a call from God. Good-heartedness and activism are not enough. For Moses it was a case of instant burn-out; he gave up the struggle and ran for it. It was as though he went into retreat for forty years, living a slow-moving life, with time to sit around by wells, open to anything that might happen.

That is a dimension of life that many of us find very difficult. Tilden Edwards tells the story of an RE teacher at a Christian private school who decided to introduce silent meditation into one of his classes. He told the pupils simply to 'be' during the silence: to be

59

relaxed and awake, open to life as it is, with nothing to do but appreciate whatever comes. Edwards comments that the response of the young people was very revealing. 'One boy summarized a general feeling of the class: "It is the only time in my day when I am not expected to achieve something." The response of several irate parents was equally revealing: "It isn't Christian," said one. "I'm not paying all that tuition for my child to sit there and do nothing," proclaimed another' (*Spiritual Friend*, New York, Paulist Press 1980, p. 69).

We live in a world in which your work is measured by what you achieve. This is not just to inveigh against crude consumerist materialism. For the same kinds of attitudes seep through into every aspect of our life, into leisure, into relationships, even into prayer. Many people in pews think of prayer as though it were basically intercession or asking, persuading God to get things done. Prayer comes then to be appraised for its 'efficacy'. And even when we realize that there is a bit more to it than that, how easy it is to measure the work of prayer by the 'good feelings' or 'sense of God's presence' that we enjoy.

So it is important to have times to be idle, when we desist from achieving, from striving, from putting forth effort, from setting ourselves goals. I usually point to the importance of this at the beginning of a retreat. I suggest to the retreatants that they deliberately refrain from rushing, that they walk more slowly, that they be more aware of their surroundings, but above all that they let go of the things they have brought with them to do 'because there will be time to catch up with my letter writing or reading,' or whatever. But usually within the first few hours of arriving I notice someone walking across the hall with purposive step and a distant look in his eye, obviously miles away, with his mind set on some as yet unattained objective. The fact is that it is very difficult suddenly to change gear like that unless it is something that has a place in your daily life.

Something to do. Begin to make space for loitering in your own life, if you do not do so already. Take time to stand at your window and take in the details of the scene, whether urban or rural, however boring and uninspiring. Sit down and draw something you can see from your window. Stop for a few moments as you walk down the street or through the park or down a country lane, and listen to the sounds you can hear; or watch a bee extracting nectar from a flower. Some time in the next few days give yourself half an hour in which simply to do nothing, like the children in that class.

3. BE INFORMED ABOUT THE WORLD'S NEED AND OPEN TO OTHERS' PAIN

Read Exodus 1.8–14 and 2.11–15 and reflect on it.

The Epistle to the Hebrews (11.24–29) makes great play of Moses as one of the heroes of faith. The Exodus text is a little more down to earth. As Brevard Childs remarks (*Exodus*, SCM 1974, p. 43) in the actual text of Exodus, 'there is very little of the hero of faith who decides for God.' But the author of Hebrews is quite right about Moses refusing 'to be called a son of Pharaoh's daughter, preferring to share hardship with God's people', even if his motives are only implicit in Exodus 2.

The personal calling of God arises from the interplay between three factors: the person you hiddenly are and could be; the needs of others; and God, whose invitation to you is to put the one at the service of the other. It is therefore essential that we are well informed about the world and its people, about how people are ground down, about what prevents them from flourishing, about the appalling things we do to one another. This does mean opening our minds and hearts to the world's pain. It can be a helpful, if distressing, discipline, to recall some incident that made you aware of others' pain or oppression, and then, in a meditation with your eyes closed, to allow their distress to enter into your heart and soul. One way of doing this is, after a few minutes preparing yourself by sitting quietly and allowing the sensations of breathing to focus your attention, to picture your breath-stream as a loop within the vast network of the world's life, linking you with it. As you breathe in, allow the pain of the particular people you are thinking of to pass through your heart, and out again. You are not to hold on to the pain, or, at this stage, feel obliged to *do* anything about it. It is often the conviction that there is nothing we can do about it that prevents us allowing ourselves to feel it at all. But we cannot be open to what God would have us do unless we allow ourselves to be affected and our hearts

61

touched. Then at the end of your meditation be aware of Jesus beside you, opening his heart to this situation: and talk to him about your feelings and reactions (there is a fuller guided meditation along these lines on a cassette obtainable from JIJO Tapes, c/o The Warden, Education Resources Centre, The Old Deanery, Wells, BA5 2UG).

That is a way to begin to educate our hearts. Our minds also need educating. 'A man's eyes', says one of Charles Kingsley's characters, in a discussion about poverty, 'can only see what they have learned to see.' And many vested interests in our land and across the world have powerful motives for making sure that we do not learn to see.

In the course of preparing to write this book I asked a series of questions of a lot of ordinands and would-be ordinands. One of them was, 'Who are the people you particularly want to concern yourself with or minister to?' Many of the replies were extremely vague about this. Many candidates seemed to have given little or no thought to the actual people they would be working among. Even if they had, I got the impression that what they would be offering would be a pre-packaged message, without much knowledge or understanding of the recipients. This was not true of all my respondents, but it was alarmingly widespread. It is an attitude that seems to me to be around rather commonly in the Church. What often seems not to be realized is that the goodness of the news very much depends on the circumstances of the recipients. It depends at least as much on the recipients as on the announcer. For example, for the oppressed and the ground down, good news would be freedom and self-determination. For the rejected, that they are valued or loved. For the bored and the trapped, some sense of meaning and purpose. For wage slaves, creative activity that connects with who they really are. For the spiritually starved, intimations of God. And so on.

Something to do. Meditate on Luke 4.18–19. Begin to make a list of people who are in some way or another impoverished or imprisoned, oppressed or without sight. As you make your list in odd moments over several days, notice the ones who touch your heart most, the people or situations you are most concerned about. How could you put yourself in the way of receiving from them? – or listening to them? – or sitting where they sit?

4. WHAT KIND OF GOD?

Read Exodus 2.23—3.10 and reflect on it.

'Who you are and where you are play a quite critical part in determining the God whom you meet. On the Manor (a Sheffield housing estate) amid the poverty and deprivation of that place God meets us who are affluent in the persons of his poor to challenge all the assumptions of our mainstream culture: they challenge our materialism (that's the bad news of the gospel) and they allow us to admit to weakness and vulnerability and failure in a culture that speaks only of success (and that is the gospel of God for affluent people)' (Alan Billings, in an article in *Southwell and Oxford Papers on Contemporary Society*, September 1989).

We all have biases in our notions of God. Some of these come from the culture or social milieu in which we have been brought up. Some come from the kind of church background we had. For example, Moira's parents were devout Roman Catholics. There was in her background much genuine emphasis on prayer and finding out what God wanted you to do. But there was no doubt about what the highest vocation was for a woman, and that was to be a nun. As a family they got to know several nuns in a nearby community, and Moira came to like and respect one of them in particular who – improbably, considering this was the fifties – taught political science. She seemed to her a 'really nice mixture of holiness and living in the world'. At the age of eighteen Moira joined the order, with the strong sense that this was the will of God for her. Ten years later she was beginning to realize that her family's view of perfection and of God's will was a somewhat blinkered one. Eventually she left the order, and looking back she can see that it was partly as a result of the pain and confusion of having to revise deeply held values that she later became a psychotherapist. But even now, more than twenty years later, she still feels that all this has left a deep impression on her attitudes to God and religion. She still finds it difficult to think of God and the will of God without feeling she is becoming entangled again in all those assumptions.

Some of our notions about God have more to do with the general attitudes of our parents outside the sphere of religion, in the narrow sense of the word. For instance, in my own youth one of our family precepts was, 'Try very, very hard, but don't succeed because that will lead to pride, which is the worst sin of all.' I don't remember this ever actually being said. It was one of those things that sort of hung invisibly in the atmosphere at home and which I absorbed unconsciously through the mere process of breathing. Only decades later did I begin to notice that I was sometimes prone to what you might call the Sisyphus syndrome. Sisyphus was the gent in Greek mythology who was condemned to spend his life rolling a huge stone up a steep hillside; and every time, just as he was about to get it to the top, it would roll down again. With hindsight I can see how much this influenced my idea of God. I saw God as a sort of celestial slave-driver. You always had to try very hard in order to get approval, and even if you did get it, it would be of the form, 'Well done, good and faithful *servant*' – it might just as well have been, 'Well done, good and faithful *slave.*' I think one of the reasons I so much wanted not to be ordained was because something in me of a more healthy disposition wanted to keep out of the light of this oppressive God, though I was not aware of it at the time – the health of the disposition, I mean. At that time I would have called it a sinful disposition. I simply assumed that God was actually a slave-driver: it never occurred to me to question this assumption.

So in this section I am pointing to the need to increase our capacity to be open to God as (s)he is, and to her loving invitation to each of us to offer ourselves and our energies so that others may flourish. Does that surprise you – the pronouns, I mean? Some of us are so used to 'he' and 'him', with or without capital letters, that we have ceased to realize that any ascription of gender to God is metaphorical. Nor is this notion a merely modern one. The fourteenth-century mystic, Julian of Norwich, writes, 'God is as really our Mother as he is our Father' (*Revelations of Divine Love*, chapter 59). 'In our Father, God almighty, we have our being. In our merciful Mother we have reformation and renewal, and our separate parts are integrated . . . In yielding to the gracious impulse of the Holy Spirit we are made perfect' (chapter 58).

Perhaps because it is so apt a notion, it is easy to forget that the ascription of parenthood, Father or Mother, to God is also a metaphor. In our growing understanding of God throughout our lives it is important to peel away from our perception both the qualities we impute to God because of the influence of our upbringing, and also the cultural assumptions that we are imbued with. Part of what spiritual growth means is the gradual shedding of defective or blinkered notions of what God is like, in order to increase our openness to the reality of God, who is beyond our understanding and who can never be contained by our metaphors and comparisons. In saying this, though, I am not just talking about the God you say you believe in, the conscious beliefs of your intellect. I am talking about the God that others might infer that you believe in, judging from your attitudes, the way you live your life, the type of person you are. That is the faith you actually live by, as opposed to the one you think you live by, and that can be quite difficult to be aware of, and even more difficult to change.

Something to do. You could begin a little self-examination in this area by asking yourself: if they were to judge by my attitudes, what sort of God do my friends think I believe in? – does my partner think I believe in? – do the people who I disagree with or who are critical of me think I believe in?

5. YOUR GIFTS

Read Exodus 4.10–11, preferably in a inclusive language version, and reflect on it.

'How dare you despise what God has made!' wrote Harry Williams. Self-depreciation is very widespread and is actually approved of in some Christian circles. Humility is something different, a willingness to accept yourself as you are, your gifts as well as your flaws.

Talk of gifts can be very off-putting. So often they are taken to mean artistic gifts or at least very special gifts which 99 per cent of us do not have. In some Christian circles they are assumed to mean only the ones listed in Romans 12, 1 Corinthians 12, and Ephesians 4. For very many of us any talk of gifts immediately raises our conviction that we lack them. Often this is because of low self-esteem, sometimes exacerbated by experiences in school when we were young when the message came over strongly, 'You're no good, you have no abilities.' But sometimes it is also a half-conscious cop out, because if I accept that I have a gift, that puts an obligation on me to exercise it: hiding our gifts can, we imagine, make for an easier life.

One of the really unconstructive features of the old *Book of Common Prayer* is its relentless emphasis on our unworthiness and the way it encourages what Harry Williams calls 'the good orthodox grovel'. Used in the context of today's culture and assumptions the BCP encourages that kind of cop out. Hugh of St Victor, who pre-dated the BCP by some five hundred years, wrote: 'Love yourself because you are loved by Him. Delight in His gifts because they have been given by Him' (*The Soul's Betrothal-Gift*, Dacre Press 1945, p. 13).

But beware of thinking of gifts as though they were separable from you, as though they were optional bolt-on extras which some have more than their fair share of. Basically your gift is you. It is *you* that is to be a gift in what you do. It is the unique person that you are in yourself that God calls you to give in action. To talk of gifts can arouse expectations that you must search for qualities or capacities within yourself that easily accept pre-formed labels. That was the initial assumption of a friend who is training for ordination; but she soon saw beyond it:

> I do not have gifts in music, or in working with young people and children; I do not have great oratory powers; I am not good at administrative work; I am not quick thinking or very organized in my thoughts or daily life. But I know what it is to laugh and cry; to love and to hate; to suffer pain and disappointment, grief and barren despair. I know what it is to sin and to know God's forgiveness; to feel bitter regret, and then peace and hope in him. I know what it is like to be an atheist and a believer, and the struggle involved in both. This is all I can offer, along with sincerity of nature and a personality which does nothing half-heartedly and never gives up.

Knowing your gifts is of course not the same as hearing a call. Being aware that you have a gift for getting alongside people says nothing about who God is calling you to be alongside, or how. Nevertheless becoming more aware of your gifts and exercising them more consciously is certainly a start on the journey of personal calling. It is important to know what you are good at, and to make space for that in your life. If you never express your own *joie de vivre* in doing what you love to do, you run the risk of becoming one of those killjoys who is always stopping others doing so. Even doing so yourself is no guarantee that you will not sometimes stand in other people's way. Another friend who plays the guitar remembers when he was a teenager withholding some information about a progression of chords from other members of his youth club. Maybe we all do that kind of thing at times. When I catch myself at it, I need to ask myself, 'Am I really exercising my own gift in freedom, or am I using a certain natural ability to bolster a weak self-esteem or to maintain power and influence over others? Am I afraid of losing something by giving and sharing what I have?' If so, I need to discover or to know once again that I am loved and accepted by God. There can be no genuine sharing of gifts unless a person is well and truly grounded in the love of God. When ego-boosting is the name of the game, both God and gift depart.

The fact is that most of us only live a fraction of what we are capable of, so we are all prone to that kind of obstruction of others. The root of it is sometimes a form of envy, as much as to say, 'If I'm not having a great time, why should you?', though it is not usually as conscious as that. You may not even be aware that you are 'missing something'.

For your exploration of your own undiscovered potential, your own unlived gifts, you could do worse than make use of the acceptable face of envy, namely admiration. The qualities you particularly admire in others are often ones you have within yourself but are not exercising as fully as you are capable of. This is to make positive use of the phenomenon called 'projection', which is universal among human beings. Since we shall refer to it a number of times later on in the book I will explain it briefly here. Jesus explained it best, and with a lovely touch of humour:

> Why do you look at the speck in your brother's eye, with never a thought for the plank in your own? How can you say to your brother, 'Brother, let me take the speck out of your eye', when you are blind to the plank in your own? You hypocrite! First take the plank out of your own eye, and then you will see clearly to take the speck out of your brother's.
>
> (Luke 6.41–42)

Projection is the process by which we see and criticize faults in other people as a way of avoiding awareness of the same faults in ourselves. So for example by looking down on another person for being two-faced we can make ourselves feel really honest and straight compared with him and can kid ourselves that we are never guilty of such duplicity ourselves. The things that most tend to get your goat in other people are traits that you exhibit yourself. The process is usually unconscious. We are usually unaware of doing this; which is what makes Jesus' description so accurate and amusing. We reckon we can see *so* clearly.

'Projection' is shorthand for this universal human tendency to blame our own faults on others in this very specific kind of way. But for our purpose just now we need to notice that we also 'project' our unacknowledged good qualities. Projection also operates in a good and positive sense: the qualities and capabilities we particularly admire in others are ones for which we ourselves have some hidden potential.

Something to do. So here is something to do to make positive use of this quirk of human life. Think of people you admire, acquaintances, famous people, historical figures, fictional characters, anyone. Then make a list of the specific things you admire about them, their qualities and what they do. Your list will then be a kind of prospectus of the unlived life that is hidden away within you which God would call out in some particular and specific way for the enrichment of others. You are not of course called to be a clone of the person you admire. In any case one does not usually admire everything about a person. But what you do admire is at least a clue, a pointer to your own unlived capacity.

I should add here that we also need confirmation from others. I would never have discovered I had any gift for writing, for example, if other people had not pointed it out. We need to be patrons of one another's gifts. Why not suggest doing some form of gift-naming exercise in your house-group? (A way of doing this is described in *Live for a Change*, 2nd edn, pp. 99–101.)

6. LAW OR GRACE?

Read Numbers 13.25—14.11 and reflect on it.

When I was young I assumed that all the biblical material about the promised land was to be cashed Christianly in terms of a land beyond the grave. It would never have occurred to me to think it had anything whatever to say about this life, except to remind us that life on earth is a vale of tears to prepare us for that new land.

Deep within each of us is the hope for a new land, a bright future, a better life. It may get trivialized into a new car or a cottage in the country, but that longing is present in everyone, however camouflaged or distorted. That is why advertisers who subliminally key into it are so successful. At bottom it is the longing for the promised land, the Kingdom of God. It is very important to do justice both to the longing and to the promise of the Kingdom to which God calls us, and to recognize that this call is for *now*, for this life. We need to allow ourselves to feel the longing in all its unfulfilled pain and in doing so to begin to hear how we are to begin to live its fulfilment. The person who is living their response to God's personal call is already in a sense participating in the life of the Kingdom. But the new land is populated by giants, the treasure is hedged about with thorns, the tree of life is guarded by a sword, whirling and flashing. That is why we try and settle for less. We fear the cost will be too great. Numbers 13 and 14 is a powerful parable of the truth about backsliding humanity. But there are Calebs around, Kingdom people, people who are living their calling. Deep *within* each of us also is a Caleb, whose longing is undiminished and who knows the promise is true and that if we step out God will be with us.

It is really a matter of whether we live and work under the law, or whether we accept God's invitation into the realm of grace. For example, Robert Tear describes the masterclasses he gives for young singers:

> Having little idea of mortality they saunter and laze both in mind and spirit ... They arrive at my class but half-awake, half-prepared, dead in the head and half-alive in the voice. They then rest their lazy souls and perform constant cliché ... They conceal the basic self, hiding from possible embarrassment and hurt in a shell of received interpretation. Perhaps these qualities arrive later, like essence after bottling, perhaps they don't rest in some souls. My task, and this is hard physical and emotional work, believe me, is to create in these pretty people, possibilities, awarenesses. I must force their unwilling bodies into real situations. I must ignite the fuel of their imaginations. All this is truly possible and the most amazing results are suddenly upon you. Deep personal feelings are liberated, the piano becomes white hot with electricity, it is untouchable. Limbs are suddenly freed. The dull theatre turns a phosphorescent gold. The world reverses on its axis. Next time most are back to the crutches of cliché.
>
> (*Tear Here*, Deutsch 1990, pp. 158–9)

In my view to be under the law means to play safe, to do what is expected of you, to stick to the rules, and on no account risk 'losing your life' (Luke 9.24). To live with grace means to do what you love to do and to put your heart and soul into it, to risk everything to enter the land the Lord your God offers you. 'The Kingdom of Heaven is like treasure which a man found buried in a field. He buried it again, and in joy went and sold everything he had, and bought that field' (Matt. 13.44).

Something to do. Think back over the last few weeks or months; what have you done that you have found especially fulfilling or energizing? Have there been any times when you felt you were doing what you are for, when you have had a strong sense of going with the grain of your being? Make a list of things that you have done that have had this quality about them, things that you are pleased with, that have made you feel more alive.

If you really cannot think of anything at all, then imagine you have been given only twelve months to live. For ten of those months you will be able to live an active life. How will you spend the time left to you?

7. DREAM DREAMS FOR OTHERS

Read Exodus 3.16–22 and reflect on it.

A friend who works in a firm 'inimical to Christian values' wrote:

> I dream of the day when one worker will use another with courtesy and find courtesy in return; when credit is given where credit is due; when those falling short of standards are helped to understand how, why, where – indeed, what those standards are; when the standards themselves are those of quality and excellence and good service. I dream of the day when those who work for my firm – for any firm – would be proud to do so, because the firm itself has a reputation among its customers; when the customer gets from us the thing which is exactly what he wanted; when the deal was so much to our mutual advantage that the next time he wants to buy, we are his natural first thought. I long passionately for these things, and for the sweeping spiritual renewal which has to precede them. I fear for the people; they are in a state of post-Christian darkness; darker than ignorance because they have turned away from the light they once knew . . . I had to pause there for tears: I'd nearly found myself typing 'O, my people, come back to me . . .' So many people I know seem to feel that God is an invention of mankind's, to help us cope when we couldn't

manage alone. Now we have grown up we can dispense with such childish things. I have seen and heard so much of this attitude that it makes me welcome with open arms the folk religion which others view with doubt and dismay.

Each of us is vouchsafed a tiny little part of God's dream for the world. God lifts the corner of the curtain to give us a glimpse of the land that (s)he longs to give us. We need to nurture that bit of God's longing deep within us, to allow ourselves to feel God's love and compassion for people, and to dream God's dream for them.

Something to do. Look back to your reflections in section 3 of this chapter. Who were the people who touched your heart most, the situations you were most concerned about? What would you like to see happen for them? What would it be for them to flourish? Dream a dream for them. If it is slow to come, take your time, and take encouragement from Habakkuk: 'I shall stand at my post, I shall take up my position on the watchtower, keeping a look out to learn what he says to me, how he responds to my complaint. The Lord gives me this answer: write down a vision, inscribe it clearly on tablets, so that it may be read at a glance. There is still a vision for the appointed time; it will testify to the destined hour and will not prove false. Though it delays, wait for it, for it will surely come before too long' (2.1–3). Do what he says; don't be afraid to write down any glimmerings you might have. Often fear stands in the way of this process. We are afraid to sound foolish or arrogant for thinking such thoughts, even in the privacy of our own journal or notebook. In so many ways have we been discouraged from building castles in the air. But unless they first take shape in your mind's eye and begin to kindle your longing, they haven't a chance in the rough and tumble of life. So, dare to dream. And as your dream begins to become clear and somehow won't go away, find someone you trust who will listen to your dream. And notice how you feel as you tell it.

8. PONDER ON THE POSSIBILITY OF A PERSONAL CALL TO YOU

Read Exodus 3.7–12a and reflect on it.

From the answers which many ordinands and would-be ordinands have been good enough to give to my questions I have to say that the impression I get is that most of them have not done any work at all on personal calling. Like Robert Tear's would-be singers they 'saunter and laze in mind and spirit' in the assumption that their personal call is to be ordained. Many of them are so young that they have not lived enough really to understand what I am talking about in these pages. A few of my respondents articulated a genuine enthusiasm for some task that obviously connected with their own deeps, but it seemed they had not thought about it in terms of what God might be calling them to offer to *others*. Many described activities that they enjoyed, but most of these were of the ready-made variety, filling pre-existent slots of one kind or another, and nearly all of these were churchy slots. I am not trying to be unkind or rude in pointing all this out, just provocative. I think the whole Church needs waking up about the business of personal calling, and therefore would-be ordinands and their mentors do too. If the future clergy and leaders of the Church have not done any work on it, God help the rest of us!

If that last remark sounds odd coming from one who is a clergyman himself, let me say that I see myself first as a lay person, and secondly as a priest. If you are one of those who has aspirations – or fears, as the case may be – that you are for ordination, please take note of this. When you are ordained, you too will be a lay Christian first, an ordained one second. So my task is to encourage you to do some work now on the issue of personal calling.

It may be that so far you are totally bemused by all this talk of personal calling. You may not have the foggiest idea about God's personal call to you. That would not be surprising, for some of the reasons I have mentioned in previous chapters. It is very important to be patient, to wait on God, not in mental slumber, but with watchful eyes and ears and a listening heart. Usually we do not hear because our attention is far too narrow and far too selective. And when we search, we are so little acquainted with ourselves, and our notions of God are so narrow, that we look in the wrong places.

Three stories to reflect on. There is a Sufi story about the Mulla Nasrudin. He was with his students one day, and was filling a large pitcher with a bucket. He drew one bucketful and poured it in. Then another. As he was pouring the third one in one of the students could contain himself no longer: 'Mulla, the water is running out.

That pitcher has a hole in the bottom.' Nasrudin glared at him. 'I am trying to *fill* the pitcher. In order to see when it is full my eyes are fixed on the *neck*, not the bottom. When I see the water rise to the neck the pitcher will be full. What has the bottom got to do with it? When I am interested in the bottom of the pitcher then only will I look at it . . .' (Idries Shah, *The Exploits of the Incomparable Mulla Nasrudin*, Jonathan Cape 1966, p. 54).

Jenny came on a course on personal vocation some years ago, because she had felt for a long time as though God had something for her to do. But she had no idea what, and half expected

> . . . it couldn't happen to me. As we did the exercises and explored the ideas I remember thinking I would never get there because I hadn't a clue what his call to me was. Perhaps there wasn't one for me. I certainly didn't think I had any gifts to offer. I almost felt in a panic as other people seemed to know what they were about. I remember saying in my small group that I wanted a letter from God saying, 'Dear Jenny, I am inviting you to apply for the position of . . . You don't have to do it, but it's what I want for you. Love, God.' And I still had no idea when we'd finished. I didn't for a long time while attending the follow-up sessions. And I don't quite know when it became more positive. It's just crept up on me. When I look back at my journal I see very little of the events that led to it. Three were, with hindsight, particularly significant. There were all sorts of things I did mention around that time. Why did I miss these three out?

A story from Anthony de Mello's *One Minute Wisdom*:

> Even though it was the Master's day of silence, a traveller begged for a word of wisdom that would guide him through life's journey. The Master nodded affably, took a sheet of paper and wrote a single word on it: 'Awareness.' The visitor was perplexed. 'That's too brief. Would you please expand on it a bit?' The Master took the paper back and wrote: 'Awareness, Awareness, Awareness.' 'But what do these words *mean?*' asked the stranger helplessly. The Master reached out for the paper and wrote: 'Awareness, Awareness, Awareness means AWARENESS'.
>
> (p. 10)

Something to do. Look again at your dream from the last section. What practical step could you take towards it, however small? Take that step, and afterwards write in your journal about your feelings as you did so.

It may be that you have got yourself so focused on ordination that you cannot think outside that framework. If so:

a) Reflect on the kind of people you would be particularly concerned about or interested in if you were to be ordained.

b) Reflect on what you love to do most, regardless of whether you see it as connected with being ordained or not.

c) How could this activity of yours be used to enrich the lives of those people? Think of one or two hare-brained possibilities. If your sense of calling is about wanting to see changes in the nature of the ordained ministry itself, think in some detail about what you would like to see.

d) Is there a step you could take towards one of these possibilities in your present position, without waiting to be ordained?

e) If not, what's stopping you? Ask yourself that question several times: and answer it as honestly as you can. Are these barriers really as insurmountable as you think? Or is it really that you are afraid of the work involved? Or the risk?

Find one or two other godly and perceptive people and talk over with them the issues these questions have raised for you – but only *after* you have worked with them yourself!

5

Call in the Bible

'Confirmation came and went and things seemed to settle down, and I almost dismissed the idea of calling', wrote Karen (see pp. 18–19):

> But then, an unfamiliar and violent spiritual upheaval developed inside me. It felt as though someone was kicking me about inside my chest. It hurt, it wanted to be released and it made me wonder if God was playing football inside there. It got to the point that I ran away to look for God in solitude, as always following the river knowing that I could cry and scream without being overheard if the occasion might arise.
>
> I walked for some time in silence and great distress. Then I started to cry. I sat down on a rock and found myself saying 'No! I can't. I won't! Please don't make me!' I was screaming and sobbing and completely absorbed by the conversation that was evidently taking place, until eventually it dawned on me that I didn't really know what I was arguing so vehemently against. Some part of me must have done, but I had no access to this.
>
> I fell quiet and decided to listen. This listening took the form of a kind of diagnostic scanning what in my thoughts related to this emotion. I sorted through the debris in my brain and soon came across the word ordination. Before it had even formed itself properly I knew that this was it. And it sparked off a fresh bout of wailing and complaining. I thought God was being totally unreasonable and unrealistic. The battering in my chest was getting worse all the time, until it became unbearable. I couldn't take any more. I slumped and gave in to God and said, 'Yes.'
>
> This 'Yes', which was a firm commitment, had been squeezed out of me by great force. It was rather a curious position, because I had only said 'Yes' to stop God from assaulting me so mercilessly. I also realized that God was not to be trifled with and that 'Yes' meant just exactly what it said.
>
> It all seems unnecessarily dramatic, but it was in fact a brilliant move on God's part, because it got me where I needed to be; totally at a loss, helpless and completely dependent on God. Ordinarily I would have taken myself and the situation in hand and would have gone ahead self-confidently, listening to no one but myself. As it stood I knew that I was going to be led by God, and maybe by other people.

I quote this part of Karen's story at some length because it is an example of a universal theme in our relationship with God. It is not peculiar to Karen, except perhaps that she is unusually articulate about it. It is the Jacob experience, the wrestling with God until the break of day (Gen. 32.23–32), a bout which leaves Jacob with, I suspect, a permanent disability, which is a kind of symbol of the dependence on God that Karen speaks of and that is required if we are to be responsive.

Since this example is not only a clear parallel to a well-known biblical call incident (see also Gen. 28.13–15) but also graphically illustrates how the personal calling issue so easily comes to be overridden and appropriated by ordination, and also because Karen is so very articulate about it, I will quote some more. First, let me say that it does seem to me that she latched on to ordination as a way of focusing her sense that God was calling her in some way. When she was casting about in her mind for a focus for her protest, ordination presented itself. I think it was for her a symbol. In actual fact at that time she did not approve of the ordination of women. It was as though ordination presented itself as a way of trying to make sense of this otherwise shadowy battle. For in these situations our adversary is God, whose ways are not our ways and whose thoughts are not our thoughts. We fight we know not what, yet for all (s)he overpowers us (s)he is life-giver and loving creator.

Karen is now sure that she should offer herself for ordination. Whether she is accepted or not will, of course, be for the Church's selection process to decide. But the real issue in all this is, I believe, God's personal calling to her; and that will be an issue for her *whether she is ordained or not*. Karen continues:

> From the age of twelve one of the few places where I felt actually alive was in the Alps, enduring all kinds of hardship, risking my life to reach the tops. There my heart, if not my thoughts, would turn to God. I couldn't allow this, because at that time I didn't believe in God. But nevertheless I met him everywhere and was drawn to him like a magnet. Back at home I used to pine for him.
>
> At eighteen I made a solitary journey over the Swiss Alps and after that I felt compelled to pursue the career of Alpine mountaineering guide. It was probably quite unrealistic and my budding career was cut short by a disabling problem with my leg. However, I remember vividly that my idea was to open up this Alpine world, these tops, to people who were frightened, who lacked trust and confidence, who wanted to get to the tops and enjoy the beauty but didn't feel they could. It was at the same

time that I had notions of being a journalist which were even more unrealistic, because I couldn't write.

Looking at it now, I think it was all about guiding people, God and communication in some sort of symbolic way. The interesting thing is that the Alpine journey, which I rarely recall, started to intrude upon my consciousness as though it was of great significance as I began to hear the call to ordination. All those years ago in the Alps the solitude and the vastness of nature must have worn down my defences, my ego, far enough for me to hear a call. I didn't interpret or understand it correctly because I didn't believe in God, or rather I used to talk myself out of my encounters with God. It just completely bowls me over to think that all those years God has been so closely at my side calling me. And all the time I either couldn't hear or wouldn't listen. Only time will tell whether my hearing has improved by now.

Karen is a person of tremendous courage and integrity, as you can see. It does sound to me as though she is right about her calling being something to do with being a guide to people in their search for God. But before you jump on me and say, 'There you are, her personal calling is to ordination! It just proves you're wrong in trying to make out that there isn't a direct connection between an inner sense of call and ordination', may I remind you that two of the best known spiritual guides in England in recent years were lay people, Evelyn Underhill and Friedrich von Hügel. There is absolutely no reason whatever why you should be ordained to be a spiritual guide. One of the things I long for is for lay people to exercise this kind of gift much more widely. It is something for which many clergy have no aptitude. There is no reason why they should, as long as *someone* exercises it.

I have called this chapter 'Call in the Bible', but the example of Karen is so apt and so articulate about the 'Jacob wrestling' element that it was worth quoting her at length. I promise I will not do this with the other elements! All I want to do is quite briefly to point to some typical features of personal calling as they appear in the Bible, so that you can ponder over them yourself and gain illumination and encouragement on your own journey. But as you do so, do bear in mind that your understanding of call in the Bible will be greatly widened and deepened as you work with the issue of call in your own life. Without your own experience and some understanding of that of your contemporaries, your comprehension of the biblical examples will be distant and lifeless and you will be tempted to try merely to replicate their experience, to superimpose upon your own life the patterns exhibited in their lives. However exalted, holy or venerable those biblical characters may be, trying to copy them results in phoney Christians, propping up our second-hand lives with 'the crutches of cliché'.

In the final weeks before my ordination in 1960 we were plied with notes on the calling of Moses, Isaiah, Jeremiah, and other biblical characters. My memory may be betraying me, but I think they were all ones in whom the sense of unworthiness or inadequacy was particularly evident. That is, of course, one of the normal feelings that accompanies the calling of God, whether the call is a direct, personal one, or whether God's calling comes via the Church and is to ordination. Whatever God's call, personal or institutional, it is *God* who calls. A sense of inadequacy before the living God is natural and to be expected. If it is absent, I would suspect that the 'calling' has more of status-seeking or an ego trip about it than a genuine calling of God.

With hindsight I can see that the selection of examples we were given effectively masked the distinction between personal and institutional calling (between calling in the third and second senses outlined in chapter 1). We were, overtly at least, being prepared for the institutional role of ordained minister. But the examples we were given were people whose calling was extremely idiosyncratic or 'one-off'. They were far from being chosen and called via the 'institution'. As examples of *personal calling* they would have been very appropriate, if our theological college had been giving us a basic training as Christians. Perhaps in actual fact, so to speak under its breath, the Church *was* offering to its future ministers a sort of crash course in basic Christianity. There was precious little training in that to be had elsewhere. As Stephen, who I mentioned in chapter 3, would have said, 'How many colleges were there for the rest?' As far as living the Christian faith was concerned, most of us ordinands were as callow as could be.

The fact is that most of the call stories in the Bible are of personal, not institutional calling. One of the major themes in the Bible is that of calling; God calling individuals to be the means of calling a people to be the means of calling humanity. The part of this process that we are focusing on in the present four chapters is the personal calling of individuals. I have described the process as it is lived by ordinary people today. It is the same process, though usually writ larger, that we see in the pages of the Bible, with some typical features about it. I want to point to some of these now. You will find it a help to look up the references as we go along, to read them and reflect on them yourself.

IT IS GOD WHO CALLS

The first and most obvious feature is that it is God who calls. We do not invent our own calls. We have already seen that graphically illustrated in the case of Moses, who rushed into do-gooding without a call (Exod. 2.11–15). After that abortive sortie in his own strength came a very long period of waiting. We may imagine that it was all the longer because of the amount of ego to be tamed and subdued. Only much later would he be described as 'a man of great humility, the most humble man on earth' (Num. 12.3).

GOD IS HOLY AND RIGHTEOUS

First Isaiah (1st Isaiah is chs 1–39, 2nd Isaiah is chs 40–55, and 3rd Isaiah is chs 55–66; any good commentary will explain this) is the most articulate and expressive in describing the goodness of God. For Isaiah not only is it God who calls, but a holy and righteous God with a concern for all the people. Isaiah is given a vision of the holiness and otherness of God (Isa. 6.1–9) which he finds overwhelming. Above all it is the justice and righteousness of God that shames him and brings him to his knees. He is only too aware of the oppression and social injustice practised by his countrymen in which he himself is implicated, if only by being their fellow citizen. 'The Lord opens the indictment against the elders and officers of his people: it is you that have ravaged the vineyard; in your houses are the spoils taken from the poor. Is it nothing to you that you crush my people and grind the faces of the poor?' (Isa. 3.14–15). The message of Amos was similar, addressed to a similar situation at around the same time.

GOD'S CALL IS TO AN INFINITE VARIETY OF TASKS

The tasks to which people are called in the Bible are many and varied. Mary was called to be the mother of the Christ of God (Luke 1.26–38). Paul was called to preach the gospel to the Gentiles (Acts

22.6–21). Peter and Andrew were to be 'fishers of humankind' (Matt. 4.19). Sometimes it was a task for a lifetime, as with Moses. More often it was brief and particular. Zacchaeus was invited to give hospitality to Jesus (Luke 19.5). Ananias was called to deliver a message, and a very risky one at that (Acts 9.10–19). So were the two Marys and Salome, 'Go and tell the disciples and Peter . . .' (Mark 16.7–8). Elijah was called to anoint Hazael as King of Syria and Jehu as King of Israel (1 Kings 19.15). Pretty tall orders, neither of which he fulfilled: it was left to Elisha to do so (2 Kings 8 and 9; presumably the delay was because of Ahab's repentance after the Naboth affair). Gideon was called to save the Israelites from the depredations of the Midianites (Judg. 6.11–24). Samuel was called to anoint one of Jesse's sons as king (1 Sam. 16.1). All these assignments had an element of risk about them. There is always some kind of risk involved in responding to God's personal call. That seems to be a normal feature of it.

Some were called to be the mouthpieces of God to the people. Such was Jeremiah (1.4–10), 2nd Isaiah (49.1–6), and 3rd Isaiah (61.1–3). First Isaiah was a government adviser, not so much a civil servant as a not-so-civil critic. Amos was a messenger of God's social justice (Amos 7.14–15 records his call). Huldah gave confirmation to Josiah's reforms (2 Kings 22.14–20). Some were called to be rather than to do; Hosea was called to be in himself a sign of God's forgiving love. At least one call was only perceived with hindsight, Joseph's, to be the means of saving the infant people of God from famine (Gen. 45.5–8). Another was a call *not* to do something, namely to Balaam not to curse the Israelites for Balak (Num. 22, 23 and 24). So there is much variety in the nature and scale of each task. Since it is God who calls there is virtually no limit or constraint on what we may be asked to do.

THE PEOPLE GOD CALLS ARE OFTEN UNSUITABLE BY HUMAN STANDARDS

This is one of the typical features of personal calling. Amos had no qualifications as a prophet, no imprimatur on his message, and no rank to pull to gain credence for it. Samuel was a mere child called to pronounce judgment on his elders and betters (1 Sam. 3). Hosea's marriage was in a mess, but he was called to be the exponent of the love of God for the people (Hos. 1.2). Jeremiah was too young and too unskilled with words to convey the unwelcome message God entrusted to him (Jer. 1.4–10). Jacob was a spoilt brat with an eye for the main chance (e.g. Gen. 25.31, etc.). Gideon's clan was the weakest in his tribe and he was the most junior member in his family (Judg. 6.15). Cyrus was the unbelieving king of a heathen country (Isa. 44.28—45.6). Matthew was beyond the pale, a collector of taxes for the occupying power (Matt. 9.9). Peter and Andrew were fishermen, better with animals than people (Matt. 4.18–20). Paul was an intolerant bigot whose mission was to be to the Gentiles, of all people (Phil. 3.6). In any rogues' gallery of this kind, he really has to have the last word:

> My friends, think what sort of people you are, whom God has called. Few of you are wise by any human standard, few powerful or of noble birth. Yet to shame the wise, God has chosen what the world counts folly, and to shame what is strong, God has chosen what the world counts weakness. God has chosen things without rank or standing in the world, mere nothings, to overthrow the existing order. (1 Cor. 1.26–28)

THE CALL OF GOD BRINGS NEW AND UNEXPECTED FACETS OUT OF A PERSON'S CHARACTER

In quite a number of cases the called person is given a new name (e.g. Gen. 17.5; 35.10; Luke 1.59–63; John 1.42; Acts 13.9. See also Isa. 49.1; 62.2–4 and Rev. 2.17). Maybe one could regard that as the name of the underlying, hidden, as yet undeveloped and undisclosed person whom God calls forth. It was clearly so with Peter, and, it seems, with Paul. It was also in the case of John the Baptist whose new name/calling was explicit from birth, showing that he was to be more than just 'our Zechariah', defined and possessed by his family: hence the consternation of the friends and relations. Take note of this if you plan to be open to God's personal call to you. I remember when I resigned my parish to start my present work, my closest relative managed never to refer to the fact for at least two years, as though it hadn't happened. It was as though I had committed some unmentionable impropriety.

WE ARE TO BE DEPENDENT ON GOD

Since it is God who calls and we have to respond from moment to moment without knowing where (s)he will take us, we are to be dependent on God. Abraham is the prototype of this feature (Gen.

12.1–9), the called person as explorer and traveller into the unknown. All he has to go on is the Promise of God. One of the features of the Pentateuch (the first five books of the Old Testament) is that in each generation, at each stage, there comes a point at which the Promise is in jeopardy. That is what makes it such wonderful stuff to read, simply for its sheer story-telling quality. It has us time and again on the edge of our seats. With Abraham there were two such moments, Sarah's childlessness and the sacrifice of Isaac. The Promise that God would make Abraham's descendants as numerous as the sand on the shore looked a little improbable, first, in the light of Sarah's childlessness; and then, later, when the old man got it into his head that his only child through whom alone the line could be continued had to be sacrificed at the behest of this apparently green-eyed God. It is all part of the treatment. God calls and promises, and our longings and dreams are kindled: and with them our egos may begin to swell, and must be subdued if they are not to obstruct the fulfilment of God's promises which are far more wonderful than any self-centred imagination could possibly portray.

OUR BABY IS NOT OUR PERSONAL POSSESSION

There is much in the Abraham saga that is so true to life in the matter of calling. I have already suggested (in chapter 3) that one way of looking at your personal calling is to see it as your baby, conceived through the fertilizing power of God. So it was with the birth of Isaac. God's command to Abraham to sacrifice him is a powerful prompt to all of us that 'our baby' is not our private possession. It is God's gift to the world through us. The sacrifice of Isaac is a reminder of the requirement that we must at some point give up personal claims on our baby: that is to say that we must not over-identify with it, it must not be allowed to be the means of an ego trip. Once you have brought your baby to birth and begun to nurture it, it is very salutary to meditate on Genesis 22.

THE CALLING OF ST PAUL

As you might expect, we find the fullest example and expression of personal calling in the New Testament. Apart from Jesus himself, who is *the* example of the personal calling of God, the clearest and most articulate example is St Paul. He writes (Eph. 3.8): 'Although I am less than the least of all God's people, this grace was given to me: to preach to the Gentiles the unsearchable riches of Christ.' This is Paul's statement of his own personal calling from God. It is interesting that he does not use the word 'call' in referring to it. He uses the word 'grace'. The Greek word translated 'grace' is *kharis*. It is an unusually rich word that contains within its various meanings much of what I have been trying to convey as characteristic of the personal calling of God.

Its meanings in classical Greek are unpacked by Armitage Robinson in one of the appendices to his commentary on Ephesians. It can mean:

i)   attractiveness, e.g. gracefulness of form, graciousness of speech;
ii)   favourable regard felt towards a person;
iii)   a specific expression of such favourable regard, i.e. a favour;
iv)   the feeling produced by a favour, i.e. gratitude;
v)   as an adverb, 'for the sake of' a person or thing.

You could hardly look for a more appropriate word for personal calling, which contains every one of those meanings: i) When you see someone doing what they are born for, there is always something attractive about it, something winsome and compelling, a sort of innate joyousness or grace. It is obvious that they are at that moment doing what they were created to do. ii) and iii) God's personal call to you feels like an incredible privilege, a totally unearned gift – 'How is it that God can be so good to me?' iv) There is a deep, abiding and amazed gratitude for this. v) What you do will always be in some way a gift to others – in other words, you do what God has given you to do for the sake of them, even if its effect on them is indirect. You may not even see its effect: it is God's gift to them mediated through what you do.

St Paul uses this word *kharis* many times with reference to his calling from God to preach the universal gospel (e.g. 1 Cor. 3.10; 1 Cor. 15.10; 2 Cor. 1.12; Gal. 1.15; Gal. 2.9; Rom. 12.3; Rom. 15.15). He clearly expresses this as an inner call from God: 'I want you to know that the gospel I preached is not something that man made up. I did not receive it from any man, nor was I taught it; rather, I received it by revelation from Jesus Christ' (Gal. 1.11–12).

To summarize, then, let me list some of the features of personal calling in the Bible:

It is always God who calls.

God is holy and righteous, with a passion for social justice and fair dealing.

The tasks to which God calls people are endlessly varied and creative, and always unique and specific to the qualities and situation of the called person and to the circumstances of their time. Often it is a task that is for the freeing or liberating or empowering of others.

The people God enlists are unsuitable, not up to it by human standards.

There is always something unexpected about the call or its outworking. It draws on hidden facets of the called person.

There is always a newness inaugurated by the fulfilling of the task, part of a journey to a new land.

The tasks are either beyond the capabilities of the called person or require special courage. They are things it would be foolhardy to attempt in one's own strength. Total dependence on God is required.

Usually the first reaction of the called person is a sense of inadequacy. If this feeling is not present to start with, it usually is later when the going gets rough.

The task, the assignment, your baby, is not your personal possession to take a pride in.

What you are called by God to do will feel like an incredible and humbling privilege, an absolute joy to do, whatever pain or suffering it may bring upon you.

It may seem strange, but often the initial reaction of a person to God's personal call to them is resistance. The temptation is to run from it, to avoid it, to avert one's gaze, to fight against it. St Paul is a classic example of this.

The same features are typical of personal calling today. In all the examples I have mentioned do bear in mind that we are talking of personal calling, not institutional calling; that is to say, none of these calls was in any sense the equivalent of ordination. For example, if you have been brought up to believe that the apostles were the first bishops, beware of reading back into the New Testament the order and orders of the later Church. 'As to the call of the disciples,' writes Martin Hengel, 'in the last analysis only the call of the Old Testament prophets by the God of Israel himself is a genuine analogy' (*The Charismatic Leader and His Followers*, T. & T. Clark 1981, p. 87).

Just to make this point clearer, let me mention by way of contrast some New Testament examples of the calling to a role. Stephen, Philip, Prochorus, Nicanor, Timon, Parmenas, Nicolas of Antioch (Acts. 6.1–6) and Phoebe (Rom. 16.1) are good examples of this (see also Acts 14.23). So is Matthias, who was chosen to fill the gap left by Judas Iscariot (Acts 1.21–26). You could regard this last as the first step in the institutionalizing process, the formalizing into a role of something that was originally personal and peculiar to a particular individual. The second and subsequent generations of any community have to face this problem if it is to take root and grow, and many come to grief at this point. At this stage in the development of a community immediately after the demise of the founder, it is in danger of fizzling out, or becoming ossified, or changing into something else. That is why the function of the ordained clergy is such a crucial one in the Church, and why being a priest/minister is such a difficult tightrope to walk. More of that in the next chapter.

Before we leave this point, there are of course examples of the calling to a role in the Old Testament as well. Perhaps the most famous is David. It is worth noting that he too is branded with the 'not worth considering' tag (1 Sam. 16.11–13). The people whom God through the medium of the Church calls to be clergy are not necessarily outwardly impressive, either. Of the imposing figure of Eliab, God says to Samuel (for which you might read 'the bishops' selectors'), 'Pay no attention to his outward appearance and stature for I have rejected him. The Lord does not see as a mortal sees; mortals see only appearances but the Lord sees into the heart.' And what does God see? Not of course 'an inner sense of calling', but at the heart of the candidate the right qualities and potential for the job.

Now it may be that you are still somewhat overawed by the suggestion that there might conceivably be some features in common between God's personal calling of you and the calling of, say, Jeremiah or Hosea or John the Baptist or St Paul. So let me adduce two other personal call narratives from the Bible that sound less exalted, where human weakness is more obviously evident. One is well known, the first less so.

Nehemiah, the king's cup-bearer in Susa, brought up in exile, hears of the plight of 'those who have survived the captivity' (Neh. 1.2) in Jerusalem. 'When I heard this news, I sat and wept, mourning for several days, fasting and praying before the God of heaven.' The city is still in a broken-down state. His dream is that the walls might be rebuilt. He prays to God in penitence on behalf of his people that the king will allow him leave to go to Jerusalem. God grants his request, thus setting his seal on Nehemiah's dream. He goes to Jerusalem and, with the people who are living there, energetically sets about the task of rebuilding. Once there, he sees the way the well-to-do returned exiles from Babylon were oppressing the poorer people who had remained behind in the city:

> The common people raised a great outcry against their fellow Jews. Some complained that they had to give their sons and daughters as pledges for food to keep themselves alive; others that they were mortgaging their fields, vineyards, and homes to buy grain during the famine; still others that they were borrowing money on their fields and vineyards to pay the King's tax. 'But', they said, 'our bodily needs are the same as other people's, our children are as good as theirs; yet here we are, forcing our sons and daughters into slavery . . .' (Neh. 5.1–5)

He realizes that he too is implicated in this injustice (5.10) and calls upon 'the nobles and the magistrates' to join him in remitting these debts.

Later with Ezra he introduces religious reforms, including the forbidding of mixed marriages, in order to preserve the purity of the revelation of God entrusted to the Jewish people. William Neil comments perceptively:

> The new community of Judah, tucked away in a backwater of the Persian empire, was to be a spectacle for all the world of how a whole people could live in accordance with the revealed will of God. In the event, human nature being what it is, it was by concentration on such external trivialities as Sabbath observance, payment of tithes and performance of ritual that the post-exilic community sought to demonstrate its obedience. Moreover, by seeking to keep itself unspotted from the world, it became a harsh, intolerant unloved pariah among the nations, a people to be shunned, rather than emulated.
>
> This was far from what the prophets, even Ezekiel, the father of Judaism, had envisaged.
>
> (*One Volume Bible Commentary*, Hodder & Stoughton 1962, p. 216)

The book of Nehemiah is full of instruction in the matter of personal calling. First is his well-informed concern for his fellow-countrymen. 'Broken down cities and the increase of hopeless indebtedness both of families and of nations' has a regrettably modern ring about it. Nehemiah allows their pain and distress to touch his heart. He seeks public office, animated by generous dreams for his people, coupled with a very practical approach to getting things done. Very true to life is all the opposition this stirs up, and the craft and subtlety and energy with which he sets about the task. He is altogether a very attractive character as we meet him in the earlier chapters of his book. But what is also very true to life is his obvious shadow side. It begins to appear in his artless prayer, which first appears in 5.19, 'God, remember me favourably for all that I have done for this people!' It is the old and universal problem that for the called person the task so easily becomes an ego trip. Nehemiah's arch-enemy, Sanballat, the governor of Samaria, noticed it and accused him of trying to make himself king of Judah. There is often more than a grain of truth in what those who oppose us have to say to us!

Every dream is liable to cast a shadow in its practical outworking. William Neil in the paragraphs I quoted draws attention to that. Usually in human affairs the brighter the vision is, the darker the shadow it throws. As we begin to become aware of a personal call from God, it is very important to talk to people with human and spiritual insight and get their feedback. But if we get from them confirmation of our inner sense of calling, then we have to get into action with as much wisdom and humility as we can muster, and hope that God in his providence can make something even of our shadow-work. In the case of Nehemiah maybe

> in the providence of God the folly and myopic zeal of godly men was turned to his own good purposes. In the Persian age and that which succeeded it, Israel would have been powerless to resist the encroachment of pagan religion and philosophy and of an indifferent morality, had it not been for the protection of the spiritual wall . . . with which Nehemiah and Ezra fenced in the life of the people of God . . .
>
> (William Neil, op. cit., p. 217)

All of which goes to show that the Kingdom is not yet. In saying that, I speak also of today. We still live in the 'not-yet' time.

However much we long for the coming of the Kingdom, our best endeavours in this life cast dark shadows. However responsive we are to the calling of God, we are all under judgment, in the Christian era just as much as were the people of God in the Old Testament.

The second example I have chosen is Jonah. This book is thought to have been written in the period following the reforms of Nehemiah and Ezra. As has already been pointed out, these reforms were designed to make Jerusalem into a fortress of true faith in a wilderness of heathenism. The little book of Jonah ventures to take issue with that approach, and the author places the story in the olden days of at least two hundred years earlier, hoping the more easily to gain a hearing for his message which would have been none too popular among some of the people of his own day.

God calls Jonah (Jonah 1.2) to denounce the wickedness of Nineveh, the capital city of Assyria, the arch-enemy of Israel. But the last thing Jonah wants is to have anything whatever to do with those unspeakable heathens. What right have they to the graciousness and compassion of God (Jonah 4.1–2)? So he sets off in the opposite direction to escape the call. In the crisis of the storm at sea the outcome of the story is already foreshadowed: the heathen sailors are more genuinely godly in their attitudes than Jonah is. But Jonah is impervious to learning: he is more concerned about his own troubles and his own faithfulness to his tradition than anything or anyone else (Jonah 2). The second time round God prevails on Jonah to go and preach his denunciation. After all, it is in line with everything he personally stands for. His worst fears are realized. They respond and repent; and God relents from the punishment he had threatened through his reluctantly responsive mouthpiece. Poor Jonah, a fate worse than death!

What a salutary lesson for all of us in the matter of personal calling! No call is ever fixed or final. Our response may change us, or it may change the situation; or it may have no discernible effect whatsoever. It is God's work and the outcome is God's. Each of the tasks assigned to us is only a tiny part of God's sovereign will. All we can do is to respond and to give generously of what we are, without really having much, if any, idea of what God will make of it: and as far as in us lies to keep our egos from getting in the way. That is the most difficult bit.

One of the most helpful and expressive biblical texts on the subject of personal calling is Psalm 119. I am of course aware that in this psalm in its original context the law, statutes, and commandments of God means the Jewish law, and in its late form at that, after the Ezra-Nehemiah period. But it has down the centuries been used devotionally in a deeply Christian sense. Let me therefore end this chapter on a more personal note with a reflective meditation on a pot-pourri of verses from that psalm. Verse numbers are in brackets:

'Your hands have made me and fashioned me, O give me understanding that I may learn your commandments' (73).
> *I am of your making, my deepest nature is from you, help me to know myself even as you know me, that I may be generous with all that I am.*

'Before I was afflicted I went astray, but now I keep your word' (67).
> *Before I owned my wounds from the past, much of what I did was to avoid facing them. But now that I have turned and felt them and allowed the presence of the pain in a conscious way, I am freer to respond to your word.*

'Blessed are those . . . who walk in the law of the Lord' (1).
> *Blessed are those who follow the deepest law of their God-given nature.*

'Blessed are those who keep God's commands, and seek him with their whole heart' (2).
> *Blessed are those who have heard and responded to God's dawn-call, and allow space in their heart for their inner longing for God.*

'If only my ways were unerring towards the keeping of your statutes (5), then I should not be ashamed when I looked on all your commandments' (6).
> *If only I could be attentive to your inner call to me all the time, from moment to moment; then I should never know the depression of being untrue to you and to the gifts you have given me.*

'I will praise you with sincerity of heart, as I learn your righteous judgments' (7).
> *As I learn to be responsive to your gracious calling, my whole being is filled with joy and praise.*

'I am as glad of your word, as one who finds rich spoil' (162).
> *Your word personally calling me to be and to do is the most precious gift I could receive.*

'I will meditate on your precepts and give heed to all your ways (15), for my delight is wholly in your statutes' (16).

'I find more joy in the way of your commands than in all manner of riches' (14).
> *Following your personal calling to me brings me the most profound fulfilment.*

'I am small and of no account, but I have not forgotten your precepts' (141).

Your calling comes to everyone, even the humblest and least noticeable of people.

'It is good for me that I was afflicted so that I might learn your statutes' (71).

Facing my inner pain helps me to be more open to your leading. Encountering difficulties and 'failure' keeps my ego in check.

'The proud have dug pitfalls for me in defiance of your law' (85).

Those whose gods are status and power and who do not even guess how alienated they are from their true nature are threatened by people like me.

'Incline my heart to your commands and not to selfish gain' (36).

Let me not be seduced from your way for me by the desire for approval or prestige or power.

'My soul languishes for your salvation, but my hope is in your word' (81).

Sometimes my longing for you is eclipsed by the stresses and strains of life; it sinks right down in my heart so that I am no longer aware of it. Then I simply cling on with a naked intent, trusting in you though there seems nothing to show for it.

'Remember your word to your servant, on which you have built my hope' (49).

'I am seized with indignation at the wicked, for they have forsaken your law' (53).

It makes me so angry when power-hunger and ignorance of others' suffering or impoverishment leads to such arrogant oppression, in the public sphere, at work, or in families.

'It is time for the Lord to act, for they violate your law' (126).

They are people who are totally alienated from you and from their deeper nature.

'My eyes fail with watching for your salvation, for the fulfilment of your righteous word' (123).

The unfulfilled longing for you and for your will to be done on earth as it is in heaven is too painful. I find myself suppressing it with self-justifying activity.

'I open my mouth and draw in my breath, for I yearn for your commandments' (131).

Some time you could read the whole of Psalm 119 and pick out the verses that speak to you and expand them in your own way.

6

To the Church, with love

The purpose of this chapter is to try to outline the basic task and function of the ordained ministers of the Church and to suggest the kind of qualities that this calls for. If I am to be faithful to my brief to address, first and foremost, you the would-be ordinands, I need to tell you what will be required of you in the role of ordained leader. In doing so I cannot avoid addressing also my colleagues and, like any preacher, myself. So this chapter is a sort of open letter to my fellow clergy and to myself and to those of my readers who aspire to be clergy. But I hope it will be overheard by people up and down the country who, as it were, sit beside me in the pew each Sunday. Since resigning my parish in 1981, I have more frequently occupied pew than pulpit and that has been quite a salutary experience. It has reminded me how painful that can be at times and how powerless one can feel, which it is so easy to be unaware of when you are the vicar. So what I have to say here comes from experience on both sides of that divide.

When I come to list the qualities required it will, of course, be a personal view that I offer, without any official ecclesiastical backing; it will be a description of the kind of people I for one would like to see in charge of our parishes. But I venture to hope that I shall, at least at times, be speaking for some in the Church who have no voice, or whose voice is not heard or heeded, but whom I meet in the course of my work.

ORDAINED PEOPLE IN NON-PAROCHIAL SETTINGS

It will be as well to say something first to those who want to be ordained for work in spheres that do not involve charge of a congregation. In this chapter I shall mainly be talking about the function of the incumbent or the minister, whether stipendiary or not, who has charge of a parish congregation. That for me focuses most clearly the function of the ordained person in relation to the Christian community. I am, of course, aware that clergy do all kinds of work in other settings, as I have done myself, chaplaincy, sector ministry, non-stipendiary ministry that does not involve charge of a congregation, and so on. Some extremely valuable work is done by clergy in these settings, and I have myself in past years been actively involved in promoting the appointment of sector ministers in social responsibility and industry. But much of this work is exploratory and not at all clearly related to the Christian community, and to use it as the *basic* model of ordained ministry can cause a great deal of confusion. As I said at the end of chapter 1, I am not convinced that all exploratory forms of ministry of their essence require ordained people.

Putting ordained people into these contexts seems to me often to be a symptom of two things; first, a disabled laity. It is a practice that carries with it the notion that you need to be ordained a) to be really committed and whole-hearted, b) to be listened to by the Church and c) to be paid. In so far as these assumptions are around, they are a symptom of a disabled laity, a disordered ministry, and of topsy-turvy priorities in the Church.

Secondly, it is a symptom of a very individualistic view of ordained ministry, divorced from its proper locus in community. I suppose this has arisen partly from a sacerdotal view of priesthood which regards ordination as bestowing personal spiritual power upon the priest aside from his or her designated function in the Christian community; and partly from taking the notion of the priesthood of all believers (meaning usually the priesthood of each believer) in a very literal sense. It is as though we try to bestow personal power or charisma on our laity by ordaining them, when the real problem is a disabled and neutered notion of what it is to be a lay Christian: for in reality that power and charisma is the birthright of *every* Christian.

In my view, we shall be clearer about the appropriateness or otherwise of ordained people in various secular contexts when we begin to get ordained-ministry-in-community right. We will see more clearly when we set the Church the right way up, the laity first and the clergy as the people who service and enable them. Meanwhile, as we grope towards this, experiment is the order of the day; and it is not surprising that we have a chaotic explosion of ordained people in all kinds of spheres. So if you have it in mind yourself to offer for one of these less standard ministries, do bear in mind what I have said. In saying it, I am in no way wishing to devalue the importance of experiment in our present state of confusion.

Some of what I have just been saying will sound to you Utopian. So in what follows I shall endeavour to work from the reality of parish ministry as it is at present, while suggesting approaches to it and qualities required in its practitioners which will help us at least to begin to move in the direction of what it is surely meant to be – enabling, Kingdom-centred, servicing the laity.

THE BASIC TASK AND SKILL OF THE PARISH PRIEST

I want first, therefore, to try to describe what I believe to be the basic task and skill required of the parish priest. In chapters 2 and 3 I pointed to what seem to me to be two dimensions or phases of the Christian life. The first phase is to know that we are daughters and sons of God, accepted and loved. We are God's creation, all that we are is of God, however defaced through our own fault or the fault of others. We are loved in spite of everything, as the parable of the loving father so beautifully expresses it (Luke 15.11–32). On our part this phase requires the realism to know and acknowledge our faults and flaws, and the humility and willingness to let go in God's presence and to allow ourselves to be loved into being and selfhood and right-relatedness again.

The second phase is the movement out into action, generously risking in the kind of way I have tried to indicate, taking conscious adult responsibility for what we do, not blaming God if 'things go wrong', and not expecting God to bail us out by some sort of magic when we encounter the inevitable difficulties.

These two phases are put succinctly in John 15.4, 'Dwell in me, as I in you. No branch can bear fruit by itself, but only if it remains united with the vine; no more can you bear fruit, unless you remain united with me.' Without that deep inner relatedness and indwelling we cannot move outwards in love and giving and creative action, simply because it is too demanding; without that backing it is not possible to stand the racket. If we try to live without it we end up

93

half-alive, anxiously conserving or aggressively striving. If you do try to move out in your own strength, or simply because you feel you ought to, you will eventually burn out, give up, or become depressed. If, on the other hand, what you do is an overflowing of love and creativity, and you do it because it is what you love to do anyway, there is no limit to what you can do. 'Young men may grow weary and faint, even in their prime they may stumble and fall; but those who look to the Lord will win new strength, they will grow wings like eagles; they will run and not be weary, they will march on and never grow faint' (Isa. 40.30–31).

I believe that the task of the parish priest at its most basic is to encourage and promote an ever-deepening engagement in both these phases among the members of the local church, and to promote their common life and worship in such a way as to enable this process and not prevent or hinder it.

When you are actually in post as a parish minister you will find yourself doing all kinds of apparently mundane tasks like calling out the boiler repair man or finding someone to oversee the church-cleaning rota, anything from chairing the Board of Governors at the local school to answering the vicarage door to a mother whose little boy left his anorak in the church hall yesterday. To get some practical idea of what the work involves from day to day it is a good idea to ask if you could spend some time with your local vicar. What I want to do here is to try to help you to understand the fundamental rationale of the work of the parish clergy which can easily be obscured by the day to day demands of the job.

In his book *The Dynamics of Religion* (Darton, Longman & Todd 1978) Bruce Reed also described the task of the parish minister and the parish church in terms of two phases. He described it as enabling people to 'oscillate' between the two phases for religion to be alive and fruitful. This is such an important book for understanding parish ministry that I want to spend a little time with it here. His description of the phases is in terms of what he calls extra-dependence, where you depend on a person or object outside yourself for confirmation, protection and sustenance, and intra-dependence, where the focus of your dependence is within yourself as a responsible self-actuating adult. He says, and I believe he is right, that this oscillation is fundamental to human behaviour from childhood and right through adulthood, and that religion provides the rituals, symbols and environment in which adults, singly and together, can 'regress' to extra-dependence. He distinguishes between what he calls functional religion, where this regression is creative and allows and encourages the worshipper to move back to intra-dependence, and dysfunctional religion, where people get stuck in either the extra-dependent or the intra-dependent phase.

He writes first and foremost as a sociologist, and is at his best in his very acute observation of the life of the Church as it is in parishes up and down the country. When I read it I was still an incumbent and I found it most illuminating. As a piece of observation of what does happen it is second to none; the descriptive part should be required reading for all church leaders and all would-be clergy. The effort of having to grapple with a bit of sociological and group-work jargon is well repaid. But do beware of the prescriptive part of it, which seems to me to fall into what G. E. Moore called the naturalistic fallacy, deriving an 'ought' from an 'is'. His prescription of what *should* happen in the life of our churches is derived from what in his estimation is the best of what *does* happen, and it comes perilously close to a sort of enlightened public school religion, rather formal and rather hidden, and definitely supportive of decent behaviour in the status quo. I say this with some hesitation because it will probably lead the enthusiasts among my readers to write it off totally. And yet is is precisely the enthusiasts among us who ought to read it! I will come back to that in a moment.

My chief disagreement with him is not about the need for some form of oscillation between the two phases. It is that his version of it is somehow much too static, a pendulum-like swinging back and forth between two relatively unchanging phases. To my way of thinking he describes the phases very much as an observer, as someone watching a process from the outside. This does seem to me to miss something rather important, namely that a genuinely Christian life requires deeper and deeper movement *into* each of the phases, in the kind of way I have tried to indicate in earlier chapters, and not just a moving back and forth between them.

However, it has to be said that in practice in the average congregation the number of people who actually want to become Christian beyond a rather modest level is relatively small. In practice you do have to work with a lot of people who are functioning in the somewhat limited kind of way that Bruce Reed describes. Part of the skill of the parish priest is to work patiently and creatively with these

95

people so that the common life of the congregation does not actually hinder those who do want to go further and deeper, and also so that those who do do not tip over into some form of one-sided, one-phase Christianity.

In the life of the Church, we are working with people in the area of dependency; our job is to help them to grow towards an *adult* dependence on *God*. The words in italics are the key to this. In parish life you come across a good deal of behaviour that falls a long way short of that – a less than adult dependency on all sorts of substitutes for God. Bruce Reed has a lovely example of this:

> An Anglican curate described how he had been responsible for a weekly evening meeting in the crypt of his Church, at which visiting speakers were invited to lecture on cultural and religious subjects. One evening during the meeting a woman fainted. People on either side of her drew back and looked expectantly at the curate. Although he had no clear idea of what should be done in such circumstances, he did his best to revive the woman and eventually with help assisted her outside into the fresh air. It was only subsequently that he recalled that over half of those present were doctors and nurses from London hospitals. Although many of those in the meeting were better equipped than he was to give the aid required, their unconscious assumptions about the meeting were such that only the leader of the meeting, the priest, was seen as competent to handle the crisis. He of course endorsed their assumptions by failing to enquire, in the time-honoured formula, whether there was a doctor in the house . . .
>
> (*The Dynamics of Religion*, pp. 46–7).

You see how the unconscious and immature dependency behaviour had taken over both the audience and the curate. In effect the curate colluded with their expectations. Again and again, in all kinds of ways, that happens in our churches. Congregations and their members behave like children and the clergy frequently collude with this by playing an unhelpfully parental role – usually in order to bolster their own weak sense of worth – and the effect of this is to prevent any real growth taking place at all.

People's dependency needs do not, of course, focus only on the clergy as substitutes for God. Often they fasten on the church building, or some part of the furnishings, or the choir, or the altar, or the Bible, or Elizabethan language, or guitar groups, or Taizé chants, almost anything you can think of – except God. It really does need quite a lot of Christian maturity to be able to look past all these things to the unseen and uncreated God. The fact is we all need aids of this kind at times, vehicles to convey us towards an awareness of God. The skill of the parish priest is to recognize this dynamic and to be patient with it; as far as in one lies not to collude with it, and to help people to move beyond the substitutes towards the living God.

The equal and opposite problem is posed by the local church which fails to enable people to move into the dependency mode at all. People can sometimes be pretty resistant to that process. In some circles dependence is almost a dirty word, while self-reliance and independence is exalted above all else. The caricature of this attitude is the self-made man who worships his maker, or the Pharisee in the parable of the two men who went up to the temple to pray (Luke 18.9–14). Churches like this 'run themselves'. When an incumbent is appointed to a church composed of people like that she may have an odd feeling that somehow she is surplus to requirements.

FOLK-RELIGION

One of the most constructive aspects of Bruce Reed's book is his approach to what he calls folk-religion, and he did much to encourage parish clergy to take it more seriously. Whatever your view of what mature Christian faith and practice is, as an Anglican minister you have got to come to terms with folk-religion whether you like it or not. I must admit that I did not like it. When I was first ordained, one of the things that shocked me most were the crowds of non-church families who used to bring their babies to be 'done' on a Sunday afternoon. And we just 'did' them without any preparation or explanation of any kind. I remember feeling that it was almost blasphemous, a kind of anti-sacrament, and that what we were doing was putting the mark of the Beast on these kids (I was reading Austin Farrer's book on Revelation at the time!).

On maturer reflection it seemed to me that there were two basically unconstructive attitudes to this problem. One was just to go along with what people wanted, like we did. The other was to refuse to baptize children whose families had no real Church connection. It seems to me that, once again, the skill of the parish priest is to realize what is happening and work with it constructively: to see that non-church people who ask for baptism for their children are expressing a movement towards God, even if it is un-thought-out and barely conscious. It may be of a very low order indeed, little more in some cases than a request for a sort of ritual magic. But it is nevertheless towards and not away from God. And we who are parish clergy have to find some way of responding positively and constructively towards this; and that is no easy task.

When you come to the ordained ministry full of enthusiasm for bringing people to God and for deepening their understanding of how faith is to be related to life, it is very tempting to be impatient with folk-religion and to regard it as a waste of time. It often feels as though people whose only association with the Church is on folk-religion occasions are somehow not on the move; and in a big parish where large numbers are involved it is easy to feel that time and energy is best spent with people who do show signs of movement in relation to faith.

It is admittedly an uphill task trying to cope constructively with people at the level of folk-religion. For one thing it is hard work simply standing out there in front of a sometimes large congregation of clueless (as far as Church is concerned) people, and carrying single-handed the weight of their total childish dependency and their unconscious and primitive projection of semi-divine qualities on you (which with their conscious minds they would probably vigorously deny). One of the things I personally found particularly hard was that in those situations you are not regarded as a person at all. You are a ritual functionary and in their view you are definitely not there to make any demands on them; you are simply there to perform the prescribed ritual. And in some cases, woe betide you if you don't!

It seems to me that to work constructively with this requires of the parish minister five things. Firstly, it requires a clear-eyed perception and acceptance of those facts about a folk-religion occasion, whether it be a baptism, a wedding, a funeral, a Remembrance Day service, a civic service, a harvest festival, a carol service, or what have you.

Secondly, to be able to carry this off without due anxiety yourself, you do need to be at ease in the role of performer. I use that word without any cynicism or disparagement. It is simply a fact that that is required of you. It is a quality that is not strong in me, which is perhaps why I am so aware of the need for it!

Thirdly, it requires an ability as well as a willingness to carry the projections of the people involved and still retain your openness and your humanity. By this I mean neither rejecting them and refusing to fill this part of the role, nor allowing yourself to be taken over by them, so that you think you actually are a semi-divine being. Very many of us clergy fall into one or other of these traps. Some fall into both. It reminds me of the old story of the two church people, an Anglican and a Roman Catholic, having a conversation over coffee at some ecumenical gathering. The Anglican was heard to remark: 'You know, in the end the only real difference between you and us is that we have a pope in every parish!'

Fourthly, it is important to bear in mind that the blanket phrase 'folk-religion' covers quite a bit of variety; e.g. working-class people with a belief in God but who feel that the C of E is for middle-class people, and on the other hand middle-class people who believe in God but whose way of life is comfortable and who do not want demands made on them. For the former, folk-religion is a way of keeping the Church at arm's length, because they know 'the Church' will not really understand their way of life and the economic and industrial forces that have shaped it. For the latter, folk-religion is a way of keeping God at arm's length, lest God's demands disturb their comfortable way of life. Both these factors inhibit and prevent people developing a mature faith, but they are different in their operation. The folk-religion phenomena that look much the same on the surface easily mask these differences.

Fifthly, it requires much ingenuity and resourcefulness in handling folk-religion occasions so that the people involved are stimulated or challenged in ways that they can actually handle and respond to. Somehow or other you have got to get alongside them and devise ways that will encourage them to take a step or two further on *from where they are*. It is absolutely no use whatever treating them as though they were further on than they actually are. Hectoring them or laying down impossible requirements is counter-productive.

When we are working with people who are functioning at the level of folk-religion we are often dealing with manifestations of dependency of a particularly immature and unconscious kind. But we do not only encounter it here. It is often very much around in the life of a congregation. The average congregation usually includes people of widely varying degrees of personal and Christian maturity. The vicar and spouse will find that they are the focus of a good deal of projection (see pp. 67–8) not only from people in the local community but also from within their congregation. They may deify you – or crucify you – or both! In other words they will tend to admire in you the good qualities they are too lazy or too frightened or too squashed to own themselves, and when they want to hit out at 'fate' or God, you are conveniently there as God's representative. And much of this is unconscious: they think you really are the Archangel Gabriel or the personification of the devil! (Sometimes when there is a vicar and a curate, one, usually the former, is the baddy, and the other is the goody!) It is obvious, therefore, that the role of vicar requires qualities of maturity to be able to cope with all this, on the one hand with the phenomena of projection without being taken over by them, and on the other with the prime task of promoting an ever-deepening engagement in both phases of the Christian life among those who are ready for it, which means you need to be living both of them yourself.

All this has implications for the minimum age for ordination. My own view is that, apart from exceptional cases, people should not be ordained under thirty and should not be given charge of a parish until they are over thirty-five. Tilden Edwards writes:

> There is something new that usually begins to happen in mid-life: a sense of finitude, a sorting out of what is and isn't important in life, a fresh spiritual search or appreciation. Before this stage illusions of infinitude, ambition for a proper niche in the human community, and trust in salvation by techniques (everything will be fine with just a little more education, therapy, money, intimacy, etc.) tend to lurk behind attitudes and behaviour. By mid-life these often become at least partially burned out or relativised. An awareness of limits, unsolvable mystery, and related compassion become more real to us. (*Spiritual Friend*, p. 107)

He is speaking of spiritual directors, but it seems to me that that is a rough and ready description of the sort of level of maturity that we should be looking for in people before they are regarded as suitable to be put in charge of parishes.

THE TWO BASIC QUALITIES OF CHRISTIAN MATURITY

I said at the beginning of this chapter that I would offer a personal view of the qualities required of the ordained ministers of the Church. Before I do that let me draw attention to what are the basic qualities of Christian maturity required of any of us, whether we are ordained or lay. In the end I believe they can be reduced to two cardinal qualities: groundedness in God and a good enough sense of your own worth; and even these two are so integrally related that they almost coalesce.

By groundedness in God I mean living your life in the conscious awareness that God is the source and the goal of your life; that all that you are is from God, that you are God's creation, and that your deepest longing is for God; that you are deeply loved, more than by any human being, and infinitely more than you can love yourself, and that God's love reaches even to the farthest and darkest corners of your personality; that you are a treasure of infinite worth, to be a gift from God to others in what you do (there is a meditation cassette entitled *Being Loved by God*, obtainable from JIJO Tapes, c/o The Warden, Education Resources Centre, The Old Deanery, Wells BA5 2UG). Groundedness in God in practice means being responsive to God's double invitation, to a personal closeness with God, and to a generous offering of your very self in singing your song, bestowing your love in action.

It goes without saying that in this I mean the reality of God, and not merely the projection of your child mind – an image of the ideal parent you wish you had had, or the unconscious imprint of the less-than-perfect parents you actually had; still less a sort of tribal 'god' who legitimizes 'us' against the rest of the world, which is a projection of internal division (tribal Christians 'see' the world in terms of goodies and baddies without realizing that that is a reflection of accepted and rejected aspects of themselves). Somehow or other we need constantly to be seeking to transcend our projections, both personal and collective, in our search for the living God, and in opening ourselves to be searched for by God.

Steeping ourselves in the unfolding biblical revelation of God is a help; to see the creativity and providence of God in Genesis, bringing order out of chaos, salvation out of division, life out of death; to see the awesome and mysterious power of God in the exodus and on Sinai; to see the gracious and caring providence of God in the promise of a new land; to see God's holiness and passion for justice in 1st Isaiah and Amos; to see God's love and acceptance in Hosea; to see the universality of God in 2nd Isaiah; to see God's vulnerability in Jesus Christ; and throughout to see God's patience with the backsliding of the people, with the sheer length of time it takes to change anything in human affairs. I remember once on a parish weekend on creativity at Scargill House we did, amongst other things, a series of twenty or so playlets, based on incidents from all through the Bible dramatized and performed by small groups, under the overall title 'The Making of the People of God'. One person's comment afterwards stuck in my mind, that what it had brought home to her was the incredible patience of God.

Perhaps we first encounter all these characteristics of God in the pages of the Bible; but it is necessary also to encounter them in your own life if you are to be genuinely grounded in God. I have to admit that, speaking for myself, it was long after my ordination when I began to be personally aware of some of these characteristics. Two conclusions might be drawn from that. Either I am setting the standard too high and that all that the bishops' selectors should be looking for is potential; or that from the point of view of the health of the Church I should not have been ordained until I was a little more mature in my experience of God. I personally incline to the latter view. I think we require more than just potential in those who are appointed as our leaders. We need some actualizing of the qualities required.

The second quality required for some semblance of Christian maturity is a good enough sense of your own worth. Most of us harbour deep within us the opposite of this. We lack a sense of worth or of value and expend a good deal of energy trying to compensate for that. We try and bolster our own low self-esteem by status-seeking or by running other people down in one way or another, and 'all because [we] cannot get on with [ourselves] and have not the slightest faith that anything useful could ever come out of [our] own souls' (C. G. Jung, *Dreams*, Ark Paperbacks 1985, p. 175). Learning self-acceptance is admittedly a life-long task for most of us, which is why I say that what is required is a *good enough* sense of your own worth. What is needed at the very least is some awareness that there is a task to be done here; instead of behaving like rats in a race, to the detriment of others, of ourselves, and of any kind of genuine community – and pretending that all is well.

A medicine for this sickness is to meditate now and then on the parable of the places at the table (Luke 14.7–14). Jesus saw the guests jockeying for the important positions: he ended by saying, 'When you give a party, ask the poor, the crippled, the lame, and the blind.' As with many of Jesus' sayings, this has also an inner meaning. To enter into the spirit of this parable, think of the poor, the crippled, the lame, and the blind in your inner world. If this seems to you a strange suggestion, approach it like this. Think of the different selves you can be in different situations, the wiseacre, the show-off, the joker, the creep, the know-all, the caring pastor, the masterful leader, the timid wallflower, the helpless child, or whatever; think also of the different selves that you sometimes feel yourself to be underneath these masks, ignorant, rejected, disapproved of, unloved, clumsy, angry, sad, frightened, worthless, clever, powerful, competitive, etc. Then make a provisional list of all the different selves you are aware of in your character and within yourself, and write brief thumbnail sketches of each one – if you like, draw each one. Then close your eyes and picture a large and welcoming room with a table laid for many guests. In an ante-room, carpeted, comfortable, and similarly inviting, Jesus, who is hosting this little banquet, is ready to receive the guests. Bring to him one by one each of your many selves, all of them, but especially the ones you disapprove of or dislike or are ashamed of, and introduce them to him one at a time. Watch how he receives each one, what he does, and what he says: and let him take each one through to the other room and give them a place at the table.

I said earlier that the two cardinal qualities necessary for Christian maturity are so integrally related that they almost coalesce. Perhaps now you can see why. We grow in our capacity for self-acceptance through our experience of being loved by God. We become more open to being loved by God through being more clear-eyed about the person we are. We can be compassionate towards ourselves because of God's compassion and care towards us. We can be more loving and generous to others when we have experienced the love and the graciousness of God ourselves. And so on. You could sum it up by saying that these two qualities, groundedness in God and a good enough sense of your own worth, are essential if we are to be able to offer genuine non-possessive love for others, and particularly to 'the least of these' (Matt. 25.40). *This capacity for altruistic love is the prime requirement of a Christian and therefore of our leaders.*

In the last few paragraphs I have here and there slipped over into talking about the qualities required of ordinands. But my main concern has been to emphasize the importance of these qualities for every reasonably mature Christian. They are qualities to which we should all aspire. Ordination candidates ought to be selected from among people who already manifest these qualities to some definite degree. Let us now turn to the particular qualities required of our ordained church leaders. Bear in mind that this is a list of what I for one would like to see. You might well want to alter it or add to it. Do bear in mind also that if these are not your particular gifts and if you are not recommended for training for ordination, there is no shame in that. Different gifts are required of different members of the Body. We are not all the same, and it is together that we make up the Church of God.

FURTHER QUALITIES NEEDED IN CHURCH LEADERS

1. We shall be freeing and enabling, not constricting and controlling. When I was a parish priest I used, as I thought, to go out of my way to encourage people to take initiatives. But I had not bargained for my feelings when they started branching out in ways I hadn't suggested and didn't agree with! For example, in the mid-seventies a charismatic house-group was formed by half a dozen people in our congregation. I was distinctly dubious about that, having heard of the congregational divisions caused by a similar move in a neighbouring parish. I also felt personally threatened by it. Here were these people manifesting a godliness that I knew I fell far short of; and where did that leave me, who was supposed to be the leader of the local Christian community? In fact, not only did this group not cause any division whatever, it did a great deal for its members who as a result grew visibly over a period of time. But it was all I could do to keep my hands off it; and I simply did not have it in me to give it any encouragement.

Being an enabling leader requires a great deal of humility, a willingness for others to be more godly, more able, more 'successful' than you are, and all of that when you have, so to speak, been shoved out in front as a leader and exemplar of the Christian life, where the expectation, both yours and others', is that you will be more godly, more able, etc. People who advocate an enabling leadership style should sit down first like the tower-builder (Luke 14.28–30) and count the cost!

Even after that kind of experience I still do advocate it; and having sat in pews in recent years and having listened to many other people who suffer in pews in all sorts of churches I advocate it even more strongly.

2. We shall be people through whom others can hear the gospel. In our role as ordained people, we represent the Church and the gospel both to the local community and to the local church. As the officially designated leaders of the local church people outside the Church have a right to expect us to be embodiments of the gospel. In practice their expectations are not always realistic or helpful, either to themselves or to us. But we do need to be people who can communicate the gospel. We need to do it first by living our personal calling: in so far as we do that we become the gospel, we embody it rather than just speaking it. Secondly, we need to be able to put into ordinary language what we believe. It is no good being thoroughly orthodox in our theology if we cannot express it in language which non-church people can understand. I suspect that if we cannot, we have not *really* understood it in our own life experience. We are still using someone else's language, even if it is the language of the Bible.

We also represent the Church and the gospel to the local church. The same two capabilities are needed. This is in practice what it means to keep the local church community true to its nature and intent as I mentioned in chapter 1. There will be times when we need to preach the gospel and to live the gospel as an example to our own congregation. It is not always enough to enable others. There will be times when there is no vision, when people are ground down or wrapped up in their own concerns. There will be times when we need to help people to catch a little of God's vision for the world beyond the church porch and of a church renewed in its own life and in its responsiveness to God's call.

3. We shall be people who listen. One of the occupational hazards of being a Minister of the Word is that we become quick to speak and feel we must always have something to say. My fear is that the Decade of Evangelism, the 1990s, may have made this tendency worse. But as I pointed out earlier, what constitutes good news (evangel means good news) depends very much on the circumstances of the recipient. I would like therefore to propose a text for all evangelists, 'Everyone should be quick to listen, slow to speak . . .' (James 1.19), and to express the hope that we who are clergy will give a lead in this. Much of our quickness to speak is self-justifying. We have a vague feeling that if we do not have an answer for everything we will be letting the side down. Holding our tongues more will be difficult. It will mean learning to live at times with a feeling of ineffectiveness. But in becoming quicker to listen we shall more truly embody the spirit of Christ.

4. We shall be able to tolerate differences in people. Differences in temperament, in their needs in prayer and worship and so on. This is essential for a parish church anyway, whatever your style of leadership. If the local church is to be for the parish, and not just for the like-minded members of some sect, it has to accommodate different types.

5. We shall be able to tolerate dissidents. Elizabeth O'Connor quotes a story about Georges Gurdjieff which illustrates that we not only need to tolerate them; they have an essential part to play in our common life. Gurdjieff founded the Institute for the Harmonious Development of Man, to awaken people to the inner life:

> One of the people at the School was a Russian by the name of Rachmilevitch. Rachmilevitch was a troublemaker and a constant source of irritation to the community. He complained about everything and often threatened to leave when things were more than he could bear. One day he carried out his threat and went to Paris. This should have been an enormous relief to Gurdjieff, but to everyone's amazement Gurdjieff went to great efforts to persuade him to return. His explanation was that he needed Rachmilevitch to stir others up. 'I know no one person like him . . . who just by existence, without conscious effort, produces friction in all people around him.' Gurdjieff operated on the theory that it was necessary to see oneself without illusion and that friction brought about conflict in people which shocked them into seeing themselves.
>
> (*Journey Inward, Journey Outward*, New York, Harper & Row 1968, p. 26)

Every congregation needs a Rachmilevitch: and most do not need to import one! You will be hurt by them, probably more so than by anyone else in the congregation. But, whatever you do, do not try to neutralize or ostracize them. They are the irritants which produce the pearls among us.

6. We shall be able and willing to accept people's negative projections without retaliation. A friend said recently, 'I wish clergy would ask themselves what people's hostility was really aimed at, instead of taking it personally.' I remember once many years ago at a PCC weekend we asked everyone to write down on a small piece of paper what they thought the Church was for, and all the pieces of paper were then lumped together in the middle of the room and we each drew one out of the heap and read it out. I only remember one of them: it said simply, 'be a whipping post'. A very perceptive comment. As the leader in the local church you are the focus for that, of course, and so is your spouse: standing there and taking it does take some doing sometimes:

> When you, as a leader, offer yourself as a symbolic person around whom the rest of us work out our own salvation, you are undertaking to walk the way of the cross. As a religious leader, you will be lifted up, and the powers of darkness will be unleashed on you. When people are working their spiritual development out on you, you need clarity about where you end and the other person begins.
>
> (Celia Allison Hahn, 'Men and Women as Leaders', *Alban Institute Action Information*, March/April 1988)

It is *essential* that you have a wise friend, counsellor or confidant who is discreet and outside the parish to whom you can sound off now and then and discharge your pent-up feelings, and who will help you to distinguish between your own fault and others' projections. Sometimes we are persecuted for righteousness' sake; sometimes it is our own egos that get us into trouble. Usually we need help to discern the difference.

7. We shall be willing to ask for help, and to accept it when it is offered. It is a particularly unlovely characteristic especially of men that we assume we ought to be able to cope on our own, that it is infra dig. to ask for help. In days gone by in high church circles there used to be lists of sins in handbooks on making your confession. 'I have failed to ask for help when I needed it' ought to be added as a cardinal sin for a church leader, to be considered in any examination of conscience.

8. We shall be careful about confidentiality. This is such an obvious requirement in a pastor that you might think it hardly needs mentioning. But the fact is that many clergy are not trusted by their parishioners because it becomes known that even the most obvious confidences are not safe with them. Deciding whether what people tell you about themselves needs to be treated as confidential does need a certain amount of common sense and sensitivity. But in general I believe it is better to err on the side of keeping what you know to yourself, and in most cases that means not sharing it with your spouse either.

9. We shall be willing to allow ourselves and others to fail. One of the things people like incumbents and deans are there for, or ought to be there for, is to make it possible for others to take risks; to provide a certain background of safety so that others can try things out, and be willing ourselves to accept the responsibility when things do not work out. I am not talking about thoughtlessly idiotic schemes. I mean creative ventures where there is a co-operative understanding of what is being attempted and why, and where there is inevitably some risk. Enabling leaders are the sort of people who can allow themselves and others to fail, and so can make it possible for appropriate risks to be taken. With this also goes a willingness to listen to criticism and to accept it when it is justified. A sense of humour, the capacity to laugh at one's foibles, does make this easier. The capacity to laugh at yourself should be pretty near the top of the list of qualities that the bishops' selectors look for.

10. We shall be capable both of action and inaction. Celia Allison Hahn writes, 'While women may need to stop pondering so many things in their hearts and go out and *try* some of them, men may need to become more inward and reflective about their lives' (op. cit.) Those two capabilities to tend to coincide with gender differences. Up to now I have not explicitly drawn attention to these differences. But, as I am sure you will notice, some of the qualities I am calling for are more often manifested by women, and some more often by men. The fact is we need both feminine and masculine qualities in our church leaders, whether they are men or women. When men and women work together it can happen that we allow the members of the opposite sex to manifest our own potential contra-sexual qualities instead of working at their development within our own character. My hope would be that as church leaders, whether we are women or men, we work at developing both sides of our character, the capacity both for doing and for being, for striving and for letting be, the capacity for community and for standing alone, for togetherness and for differentiation, for standing alongside and standing apart. Men and women working side by side in ministry can be a great resource for one another in this.

11. We shall be people who are growing in our awareness of the negative side of our personality. Many of us who are clergy have an incredibly rosy idea of how we come over to others. But we all have a dark side to our nature, qualities which are the opposite of our conscious view of ourselves and of what we intend. Other people will see this long before we do. It is the sort of thing that will out in a slip of the tongue or the 'unintended' result of some action. I once heard a Remembrance Day sermon in which the preacher was waxing eloquent about how we must work together towards a new kind of world – only he said 'a new kind of war'. He was a man whose manner of dealing with people was confrontational. He liked war; though I am sure his own view of his style was that it was a co-operative and enabling one.

The worm's-eye view reveals most, the view of your subordinates and those over whom you exercise some power or authority. It would be a good exercise once every few years for the minister in charge to pluck up the courage to ask members of his or her congregation, 'What does it feel like to be a member of this congregation?' and for the members to find the courage to be direct about that, to say the positive things without flattery and the criticisms without rancour. Although this would go beyond feedback about the personality of the cleric, the fact is that in most cases he, or she, is the most important factor in the feel of a church or a congregation. Perhaps an occasional look at this would help to counterbalance this disproportionate influence, so that the congregation could begin to take more conscious responsibility for its own life where appropriate.

12. We shall be people who know that in the end the issue is an inner one. How easy it is to blame the people in our congregation for their apparent apathy, or the Church for its cock-eyed notions about vocation, or the bishops' selectors for our frustrated lives, etc., etc. Let your temptation to blame others lead to some self-examination. If I have hopes and dreams for the congregation of which I am part and all I see round me is dullness and apathy, I need to ask myself, what is it in me that blocks the realization of those hopes and dreams? If I have a vision of the kind of leadership we need in the Church, I need to ask myself how am I blocking it; do I allow others to lead at the point of their gift? Do I know my own gift and have the courage to offer and to exercise it? And so on.

13. We shall be people who can co-operate and work with others. The clergy are notoriously bad at this; which is not only bad practice but bad theology. The power of the Holy Spirit which we are promised is manifested particularly when people work together (see, for example, 1 Cor. 12; 2 Cor. 13.14; Gal. 5.22–26; Eph. 4.1–16), rather than being the personal possession of individuals working in isolation. To put it in very basic, practical terms, even just two people working together can do far more than twice what one person can do.

I sometimes ponder on why the clergy can be *so* bad at this. Is it because we have thought of the ordained ministry as a personal calling? And so it draws into its ranks a whole lot of people who are beginning to hear echoes of the personal calling of God, but God's whispers within are drowned by the demands of the role and the trappings of authority? Do we then end up with a whole collection of people whose personal calling is stunted and blocked? If so it is not surprising if we manifest all the typical negative features of people who are not living our personal calling – concern for status, a finger in every pie, power *over* people, defensiveness, envy, blocking others living their call, and so on; and none of the positive qualities associated with living your personal calling – love, generosity, willingness to be vulnerable, enthusiasm, co-operation, freeing others, power *with* rather than power *over*, etc. This, of course, is by no means true of all clergy. Far from it; but it is common enough to be a byword. I do not know if this is part of the explanation. But I do know that we can never co-operate creatively with others unless we are living our own gift. That is simply a fact of human nature.

14. We shall be able to see beyond the confines of our own parish and our own work. A friend has been much involved in getting a hospice going and has responsibility for the volunteers. She was talking with her vicar, who knew about the hospice and had visited it, about how important she felt it was to try and draw out the gifts of the volunteers in the allocation of tasks in the hospice. 'I absolutely agree,' he said; 'actually, I had you in mind for the elevens to fourteens or the Missionary Secretary.' Most institutions tend to see the world as though they were its hub. As an incumbent it is fatally easy to get sucked into the attitude that the Church is the centre round which everything else revolves. There is a great deal of pressure to concentrate more and more merely on keeping the show going. Eventually we can forget that anything else exists at all, that, for example, people go out to work and have all sorts of pressures and responsibilities and that these occupy most of their time and energy. Sometimes I wonder if at least one of the incumbent's jobs should be to discourage or protect people from becoming too involved in church chores, which can so easily pull them away from their natural sphere of ministry.

15. We shall cultivate a sense of what is important, and what is in the end not worth fighting about. It is very easy to get caught up with pet loves or pet hates and to give them disproportionate emphasis. It would help if all church leaders stood back from the work at least once each year to review their aims and the life of the local church, preferably with a 'third party', someone from outside the situation who can help us to look at ourselves and our work a little more objectively, and be with us while we set our course for the coming year. It is good to see that some prominent church leaders now do this – a good example for the rest of us.

16. It is important, if it can be made possible, for the priest or deacon to step out of the worship-leading role from time to time and sit in the congregation of his/her church. First, because it helps you to disengage a little from the role and remind yourself that you are primarily a lay person – a member of the laos (the people of God) – and only secondarily a parson. Secondly, because it gives you at least the physical sensation of sitting in the congregation at your church, and being able to view what goes on from that angle. Thirdly, because one of the hazards of leading worship for years on end is that you risk losing the capacity for worship yourself. When you are presiding you have a responsibility for what goes on. You need always to be thinking ahead to foresee and if necessary forestall clumsinesses or muddles so that things are done decently and in order. With practice you can consciously let go of this responsibility at certain places in the liturgy and move into the dependent rather than the responsible mode for a minute or two. But I sense that a lot of clergy find that quite difficult.

17. We shall beware of substituting externally-validated power for the hard-won authority that is the result of faithful discipleship. We have in the ranks of the clergy of the Church of England everything from autocrats to abdicrats. What kind of authority are we actually given? In the ordinal of *The Alternative Service Book 1980*, at the giving of the Bible to the newly ordained priest, the bishop says, 'Receive this Book, as a sign of the authority which God has given you this day to preach the gospel of Christ and to minister His Holy Sacraments.' *The Book of Common Prayer* has, 'Take thou Authority to preach the Word of God . . .' At our ordination, and here I speak as a priest, we are given authority to be the representatives of the Church of God. So that, for example, when the priest presides at the eucharist, the whole Church, which is Christ's body, is focused in the person and actions of the priest. That is a very great and humbling privilege, and of course it extends to other aspects of what it is to be a priest. It is also a great responsibility. It is perilously easy to slide from the spirit of this to the personally inflated 'L'État, c'est moi' (I *am* the State), as Louis XIV is reported to have said. It is as well to be reminded that the Church is the Body of Christ, that the priest represents Christ. In the end, our authority is the authority of Jesus, which is very different from the way authority is usually regarded. Two points need to be made here.

The first is that the authority of Jesus was not bestowed by any external institution. Nor did he have any recognized status or position. In the social and religious pecking order of the day he was a nonentity. His authority came from within: 'The people were amazed at his teaching, for, unlike the scribes, he taught with a note of authority' (Mark 1.22). That is the only genuine authority. Without that, our authority degenerates into petty officialdom or impersonation. I realize that this will not please those church men and women for whom external authority is all. I have no wish to devalue external authority. It has a vital part to play in the functioning of institutions. But without *also* the fostering and development of inner authority (which is given gradually as you are responsive to God's personal calling to you), important human and Christian values are liable to fly out of the window. We are left with a kind of totalitarianism, of Bible or of Church or of clergy.

Secondly, when the disciples were squabbling about status and places of honour, Jesus had this to say to them:

112

You know that among the Gentiles the recognized rulers lord it over their subjects, and the great make their authority felt. It shall not be so with you; among you, whoever wants to be great must be your servant. And whoever wants to be the first must be the slave of all. For the Son of Man did not come to be served but to serve, and to give his life as a ransom for many.

(Mark 10.42–45)

As clergy we are basically there to do the chores to make it possible for the people of God to get on with Kingdom work out in the world. That is why it is *so* important that clergy are responding to God's personal call to them: that is where we should derive our sense of meaning and fulfilment, and not from substitutes like rank or status. Many of our duties do put us centre stage, as it were. We need to beware, lest the power that our position gives us flatters and inflates our ego, lest we fall from building the Church of God to building ourselves or our empires (see 1 Cor. 4.7).

18. It goes without saying that we shall be people who are ourselves responding to God's double invitation. That is so fundamental that it underlies everything I have said in this chapter. I draw attention to it in this list merely for the sake of completeness, lest itemizing the trees diverts attention from the wood.

After all this you may well feel, like the Queen of Sheba visiting Solomon in all his glory, that there is no spirit left in you. You may think that I have pitched it far too high, and the old sweats among my readers will no doubt be muttering about the absurdity of requiring these sorts of standards for our clergy. But the Church requires what some regard as high academic standards – why not also high standards in appropriate leadership qualities? It is no use making jokes about the Archangel Gabriel and wallowing in self-satisfied mediocrity. After all, it is the Church of God that we are talking about, and not some third-rate company marketing fish fingers or cosmetics. 'The children of this world are wiser than the children of light . . .' Someone who had just taken over an administrative job in a voluntary organization commented after a few months, 'I never realized how much love there is in efficiency.' If only we devoted the same amount of clarity and energy in the choice of leaders for our local churches as any competent company does, we would actually manifest a good deal more love. My impression is that the bishops' selectors do take a lot of trouble over this, but their advice is not always taken. In any case all they do is to recommend a person for *training*, not for ordination. Theoretically the selection process should continue at theological college. I wonder how much this happens in practice?

Certainly, as I listen to the experiences of lay people, I often cringe inwardly as I hear how we clergy sometimes come over. How is it we can sometimes be so awful? Are we like that when we are first ordained? Or do we just gradually get like that; arrogant, opinion-ated, uncooperative, quick to speak, unable to listen, unaware of how others feel, easily threatened sometimes to the point of paranoia – a sort of mirror image of all the qualities hymned by St Paul in 1 Corinthians 13? Why is this?

I think there are possibly four contributory reasons. Firstly, many of us are not living our personal calling in either phase. On the inward side we are always having to lead worship and over the years that *can* gradually prise us away from our own praying. On the outward side, many of us are not doing enough of 'what we are born for', so there is not enough *joie de vivre* in our active life. At the very least, we should have some absorbing hobby, and not on any account let it get squeezed out or feel guilty about spending time on it. In time that *can* become a point where we begin to hear the personal calling of God, as for example with Robert and Mary in chapter 3.

Secondly, as an incumbent, you carry the weight of others' expectations and projections, which is much heavier than most people realize. Moreover, it is something you carry all the time, because you live on the job; and so does your spouse. If your identity and your sense of self-worth are not secure you run the risk of being lived by other people's projections. This I believe is the single most important factor in the warping of the character of our clergy and the breakdown of their marriages. Any leader of course gets more brickbats than bouquets, but in most other spheres people are not placed in unsupervised leadership positions so young or for so long.

Which brings me to the third reason, pointed out so trenchantly by Bishop Hensley Henson more than fifty years ago. He reckoned it was because we enjoy an 'extraordinary freedom from oversight . . . perilous security of tenure of office' and 'the absence from [our] normal experience of any effective criticism' (*Ad Clerum*, SPCK 1958, p. 191). 'Against [our] incompetence, indifference, and indolence the parishioners have practically no remedy' (p. 91). Since he wrote, of course, it has been made possible for clergy to be put in charge of parishes without the freehold; but in practice that does not seem to have made a significant difference. I do not think that anyone should be an incumbent for more than about ten years as things are. (Perhaps we should all at some point take a turn in some sector ministry, for a change and for a taste of other worlds.) If we expect them to carry this weight for longer than that then we need an effective and loving pastoring of our clergy and some proper and regular oversight of their work. You can get this for yourself if you are very determined, but most are not and anyway would be slightly ashamed to ask for it. After all, we're British, schooled to cope on our own, and our theological colleges still do not quite dispel the notion that once inducted we are the absolute monarch of our patch. 'Wait till I'm ordained . . . !' cried one young man at a vocations conference in an unguarded moment.

Fourthly, is what we see partly an exaggeration of masculine characteristics? Might the ordination of women be helping to bring a greater human wholeness to the ministry?

Some of the things I have said about how awful we can be may sound to you very cynical and very exaggerated. If you have lived in the same parish most of your life you may never have encountered any of this. It is of course by no means true of all clergy. There are many devoted, godly, loving, receptive, courteous, and efficient people in the ministry, whom it is a privilege to be with. But in my position as it were on the edge of the Church, I meet a lot of people, both clerical and lay, and what I am drawing attention to does seem to be very widespread indeed, and is often worse than is apparent on the surface. You do not know what a vicar is really like until you are a member of his or her congregation, or PCC, or work under him or her in some subordinate capacity. It goes back to what I said earlier about the worm's-eye view. The laity have a truer view of us than we do.

In these last few paragraphs I have of course been primarily addressing my fellow church members and those entrusted with the selection, training and oversight of our clergy. If you are an ordinand yourself, or you would like to be, be warned, but do not be depressed. Remember, you do not choose yourself for the ordained ministry. Nor does it depend on your personal feelings about it. 'You did not choose me: I chose you.' It is Christ in his Body, the Church, who chooses you. Rest in that assurance, and know that if you are chosen, he will be with you in your heart and beside you in those who are, please God, pastors to you.

APPENDIX

Where do you go from here?

I. IF YOU ARE WANTING TO FOLLOW UP THE QUESTION OF
PERSONAL CALLING . . .

Your vicar, parish deacon or curate should be able to help.

Some dioceses have a Vocations Adviser who can assist on any questions about the calling of God, not just ordination.

Some dioceses run courses or conferences or continuing groups on vocation in the widest sense of the word.

All dioceses have a Lay Training Adviser or Adult Education Officer who may be able to help (though there is a lot of variation in what their titles are). Names and addresses of Diocesan Officers should be obtainable from your Diocesan Office; consult the telephone directory under Church of England or the name of your diocese. In case of difficulty, contact the Vocations Officer or the Adult Education Adviser at Church House, Great Smith Street, London SW1P 3NZ. Tel 0207 898 1399 for the Vocations Officer, and 0207 898 1510/1511 for the Adult Education Advisers. The Adult Education Department has a website at www.adultlearning.co.uk. The Church of England has a website at www.cofe.anglican.org.

A spiritual friend/director will be a great help. If you have difficulty in finding a suitable person, then the Administrator, National Retreat Association, The Central Hall, 256 Bermondsey Street, London SE1 3UJ (tel. 0207 357 7736) may be able to help, or to suggest someone in your part of the country who can.

In addition to the suggestions in chapter 2, read *Spiritual Direction for Every Christian* by Gordon Jeff (SPCK 1987).

Work through *Fit for the Purpose*, a workbook on Christian vocation

117

published by St John's College, Bramcote, Nottingham, NG9 3RL.

Convene a small group of fellow Christians and work through my book *Live for a Change* (2nd edn, Darton, Longman & Todd 1999), which offers practical DIY exercises to help you to explore the question of personal calling in your own life. Or, if you wish, work through the book on your own. My *Invitations – God's calling for everyone* (SPCK 1996) is designed as a companion to it.

Go on a retreat. They come in different forms. In a directed retreat you are in silence but meet with a guide once a day. In a preached retreat, you are in silence and there is a programme of services and addresses. Other kinds of retreat may be partly in silence. If you are dubious, dip a toe in the water and go on a quiet day. The National Retreat Association provides an annual list of retreats and 'spaces and places to be' in their magazine *Retreats*.

Vocations conferences are offered by various organizations around the country for anyone, not just people seeking ordination. The Ministry Division of the Archbishops' Council collates an annual list of these, usually published in the autumn. Write to The Vocations Officer, The Ministry Division, Church House, Great Smith Street, London SW1P 3NZ.

Useful books to read are *Landmarks: an Ignatian Journey* by Margaret Silfs (Darton, Longman & Todd 1998), and *Praying the Kingdom* by Charles Elliott (Darton, Longman & Todd 1985). *Christianity and Real Life* by William E. Diehl (Philadelphia, Fortress Press 1976) is excellent if you can get it: it is written for lay people by a layman about ministry in the secular world.

2. IF YOU ARE WANTING TO LEARN MORE OF WHAT IT MEANS TO BE A CHRISTIAN . . .

Your diocesan Adult Education Officer or Lay Training Adviser will be able to help. Many dioceses offer learning opportunities for lay people. The Adult Education Advisers at Church House (address as above) will be able to tell you where to find other sources of Christian education and training.

St John's College, Nottingham, offers correspondence courses. Write to The Director of Extension Studies, St John's College, Chilwell Lane, Bramcote, Nottingham NG9 3DS. The college website is www.stjohns-nottm.ac.uk.

The thirteen Church of England Colleges of Higher Education offer programmes of part-time study leading to a Church Colleges Certificate in Religious Studies. These programmes have been specifically designed to meet the needs of church people, teachers and college students with no formal background in religious studies. For details of your nearest regional centre, contact The Principal's Secretary, Chester College, Cheyney Road, Chester CH1 4BJ (tel. 01244 375 444).

The Urban Theology Unit, 210 Abbeyfield Road, Sheffield S4 7AZ (tel. 0114 243 5342) offers various courses. Their aim is to help you think theologically about your own situation. Its website is www.utu-sheffield.demon.co.uk.

About rural issues you might find help in *Faith in the Countryside*, the report of the Archbishops' Commission on Rural Areas. You could also contact the Arthur Rank Centre, National Agricultural Centre, Stoneleigh, Kenilworth, Warwickshire CV8 2LZ.

The Secretary, The Association of Laity Centres, Scottish Churches House, Kirk Street, Dunblane FK15 0AJ, may be able to tell you where to find other kinds of opportunities for learning.

If you are interested in exploring the possibilities of life in a religious community, the *Anglican Religious Communities Yearbook* is published each year by the Canterbury Press. This will give information about all the traditional communities of the Church of England. The Administrator, National Association of Christian Communities and Networks, Woodbrooke, 1046 Bristol Road, Selly Oak, Birmingham B29 6LJ, will tell you about other kinds of communities.

3. IF YOU ARE LOOKING FOR A JOB MORE SUITED TO YOUR TEMPERAMENT . . .

Go on a Myers-Briggs workshop (see above, p. 30).

Read *Gifts Differing* by Isabel Briggs Myers (Palo Alto, CA, consulting Psychologists Press Inc. 1980). It is not as American as it sounds. *Please Understand Me* by David Keirsey and Marilyn Bates (Del Mar, Prometheus Nemesis Book Co. 1984) is rather American but has a useful questionnaire for DIY discovery of your temperament and aptitudes. In case of difficulty, both books can be obtained from the St Paul Book Centre, 133 Corporation Street, Birmingham B4 6PH.

Your local Authority Careers Service *may* be able to help. They are only statutorily required to provide for school- or college-leavers and 'young people', but about half of the local authorities in this country offer some kind of service for adults. It is worth enquiring.

If you are a graduate, your college or university provides a service to its own graduates of whatever age. Some have reciprocal arrangements with other universities or colleges.

If you are not a graduate, your local further education college can advise about possible courses, assuming you have some idea *what* you want to do.

There are private guidance agencies who advertise in the papers, but I understand they tend to be expensive and London-based.

4. IF YOU WANT TO PURSUE THE POSSIBILITY OF OFFERING YOURSELF FOR ORDINATION . . .

Talk to your vicar or chaplain at an early stage. In any case, his or her agreement is required before you start on any selection process.

Write to the Vocations Officer at Church House, Great Smith Street, London SW1P 3NZ, and ask for preliminary information about ordained ministry. They can advise on books to read. They will also be able to tell you who could help you in your own diocese.

The Church Pastoral Aid Society produces a newsletter, *On Call*, three times a year for those thinking about ordination; it is obtainable from CPAS, Athena Drive, Tachbrook Park, Warwick CV34 6NG. They also run vocation conferences.

At the other end of the churchmanship scale is the Additional Curates Society, Gordon Browning House, 8 Spitfire Road, Birmingham B24 9PB, which issues booklets and leaflets for ordinands and runs vocation conferences.

The Committee for Minority Ethnic Anglican Concerns run vocation conferences. Write to The Secretary, CMEAC, Church House, Great Smith Street, London SW1P 3NZ, for information. They will also be able to tell you about the Simon of Cyrene Theological Institute.

For women, many dioceses have Advisers for Women's Ministry.

120

There is also an organization called WATCH (Women And The Church): contact Christina Rees, Churchfield, Pudding Lane, Barley, Royston, Herts SG8 8JX. They have a part-time office at St John's Church, Waterloo Road, London SE1 8TY.

Ask if you could spend a few days alongside one of your local clergy to get a down-to-earth notion of what clergy actually spend their time doing. If you hope to become a non-stipendiary minister (NSM), or a sector minister, or a chaplain, the same applies. If you have difficulty locating one nearby, the Rural Dean (sometimes called Area Dean) will be able to tell you who the nearest one is.

Your diocese will have a Diocesan Director of Ordinands (DDO), and most have Vocations Advisers. They will be able to tell you about the diocesan selection process which precedes going to a Bishops' Selection Conference.

Don't be hustled towards ordination quicker than you feel ready to go. It has been known to happen! And do listen to what they have to say about what the Church requires of its ordination candidates.

And do read *Love's Endeavour, Love's Expense*, by W. H. Vanstone, (Darton, Longman & Todd 1977).

If you can possibly arrange it it would be valuable for you to do some kind of pre-theological college placement in a parish to get some firsthand experience of what ordained ministry involves. What follows is an account of one such, which I was fortunate enough to come across just as the manuscript of this book was going off to the publishers, and which the author, Lindsey J. Ellin, has kindly allowed me to reproduce here:

Introduction

It has been difficult for me to recall my initial feelings, hopes and expectations of ministry; things seemed to happen so fast! One moment I was applying for social work courses, and the next I was discussing the stages which were to prepare me for an ACCM [now the Ministry Division of the Archbishops' Council] selection conference. On reflection it seemed a little unreal. In recent years I have become far more accepting of challenges and directions God seems to lead me in. As with my decision to join the staff of a hostel for offenders, so with my decision to take up God's call to the life of ordained ministry – if God wanted me to do it, I would give it a go! I did not dwell much upon what it involved. My final decision was not the result of a long study of the pros and cons of ordained life.

So what had happened in those few months of arriving in a new city and new job to make me change my intended career path? What did I believe I was being called to? And what were my feelings, hopes and expectations of my future ministry? The men I worked with at the hostel had little or nothing going for them – the 'society' we share with them has very little to offer, and they themselves rarely belonged to or were loved by anyone. This experience made me more acutely aware of what this world is about and really challenged the meaning, reality and relevance of my faith. Fortunately I found my faith strengthened and felt even more strongly that the most important message our world needed to hear today is the message of hope, love, peace, the purpose of the Christian gospel.

With a renewed conviction and an increasing feeling that the gifts God had given me were being ultimately channelled in the wrong direction, I decided I needed to follow my 'selection' to its natural conclusion.

The following months before my ACCM were a welcome breathing space in which to consider more carefully what I envisaged full-time ministry to be about and what was being asked of me. I never had an idealistic view of ministry, nor an uninformed one. After graduating I had worked for a year as an assistant to a university chaplain and that had given me a preliminary insight into the pressures and demands of life in the ordained ministry, especially as I was close both to the chaplain and to his wife, who at the time was going through training for ordination. During this time I also worked alongside an Anglican nun who devoted every hour to the running of a hostel for homeless women, and this made me aware of the total giving her particular calling asked of her. However, my experience at this stage had been in more specialized ministries which were not a reflection of everyday parish life.

It was this lack of everyday parish life experience which my DDO felt needed addressing! What was life like 'on the job'? She and I felt it would be an excellent idea if I could work in a parish after my ACCM (if I got through!) and before starting training. But where? This was mentioned to my parish vicar who saw the opportunity within our own parish. We were then curateless and therefore there was a need for an extra pair of hands. The proposal was presented to the PCC who generously agreed to give me basic financial support. I was to live temporarily in the curate's house, until the new curate arrived, and for the last two months in the vicarage with the vicar and his family.

Early days

I began my placement full of expectation of all I was to experience and learn – this God richly fulfilled. I was amazed at the variety, diversity, and frustrations of parish life. Ministers had to be able to be, as St Paul says, 'all things to all men'.

Most importantly it made me face the many issues and pressures my calling would mean.

My first experience was one I had difficulty coping with. I had been used to working in a close and supportive staff team, and living in a house with friends. Although as a residential Social Worker each day was unpredictable and relatively unstructured, you still had a clear idea of what you were and were not required to do. Physically, if not emotionally, I left work at a set time and was 'free' of commitment until my next shift. Suddenly, however, I found myself alone in a large family house, with a very unstructured and flexible routine. What was I supposed to do? What exactly was my role? To whom was I accountable? After getting up to go to Morning Prayer, what next? Yes, the vicar and the Parish Deacon were very supportive and helpful and I did have specific duties. However, it was a very different kind of staff team – each one of us had very separate workloads, and our energies were directed in different areas. I found this demanded personal initiative and creativity and I was never sure I was doing the right thing. I believe ministers need a very secure relationship with God to counterbalance the lack of security day by day. I kept wanting to ask, 'Is this all right?', 'Can I do this?', 'How would you . . . ?'

I was also initially confused as to what my role was. I was a Parish Assistant, Lay Minister, or whatever title seemed most appropriate at the time! I believe that you do not need a dog-collar to serve God in an official capacity, but without one I found that often I needed a good five minutes to introduce myself and explain exactly who I was and what I was doing. One person had thought I was from the social services! This confronted me with the issue that to many people it is the vicar and not the congregation who is considered to be the Church. What I did find rewarding, however, was that people eventually accept you for who you are; relationships in churches need to be built upon trust over a period of time. I now appreciate the need on occasions to wear some appropriate form of identity – to enable others to identify who you are – at least until your face becomes familiar.

Coming to terms with a new identity

An important personal issue for me was to come to terms with who I was and what I was called to be. I have always had a certain rebellion towards being labelled or identified as a church person, as I felt this often had negative connotations. I did not want anyone making any pre-determined assumptions about me based on stereotypes and ignorance. However, this appears to be one of the hazards of the job – after all, Christ himself was constantly misunderstood. I was also very conscious at times of my age when ministering to others with far greater experience – a very humbling experience for me. Obviously in certain situations my age was a great benefit. I am also not very keen at putting myself forward, and being a leader can still feel very strange. I suppose that, just as we come to terms with what we cannot do, we must come to terms with what we can and use those gifts given to us by God.

Neither was I very keen on wearing my cassock! Many of my objections are because I feel it is out-dated and impractical. Also I do not enjoy processing. Being up front made me feel very isolated from the congregation. I felt very public and obvious, and sometimes found it difficult to relax during worship. Those occasions when I was able to sit in the congregation were a rare treat. From a personal and a theological point of view I would feel happier being more 'united' with a congregation. In my particular church much of this separation was due to the church layout, but I presume it also stems from people's understanding of priesthood. Through this I learnt the importance of sometimes having to do things because it helps other people to worship. However, there must be a fine line between this and gently challenging people in attitudes which can sometimes be unhelpful.

Another thing I learned early on was that you do not need to be obvious in ministry to serve God effectively. I had this naive pre-conception that I was required to say or do something in order to point people Godwards! I had to appreciate that it was not my own need to give or feel effective which needed satisfying, but to become wholly available to God and the needs of others. I began to realize that to follow the example of Christ is to spend time with people where they are; to listen to their joys and sorrows, to share their laughter and tears. In the early months I seemed to visit a number of dying people, and attended several funerals which revealed the redundancy of words in many situations. Faced with death and dying (a new experience) made me question what both the Christian faith and the Church had to offer in the face of death. Two books which I read at the time and found really helpful were Frank Wright's The Pastoral Nature of the Ministry *(SCM 1980), and Sheila Cassidy's* Sharing the Darkness *(Darton, Longman & Todd 1988).*

I found sharing with people brought its own pressures and burdens. Many of those I visited were lonely and isolated. It was difficult to leave a person when you knew they might be alone again for some time. How as a Christian do you stop becoming too involved? Again, I wondered what I could possibly do. Sometimes there were specific practical things that could be done, but very often all I could do was listen and pray. How could you stop going back again and again? How could you not visit someone you knew to be bitterly lonely? And where did visiting stop, because for every one person visited there must have been ten others you could visit also! What was the relative use of writing endless minutes and attending committee meetings when there seemed so much practical work to be done? I still find these issues – and no doubt will continue to do so – difficult to resolve. Indeed is there an answer? However, I do feel that my awareness of the amount of personal pain has increased. I realize that however unjust or resentful we may feel about this, unfortunately it is something inherent in a sinful world. The temptation is to try and believe you can alleviate all the pain and suffering you find, and in the process wear yourself out both physically and mentally, rendering yourself no use to anyone. It is difficult to accept that there are things you cannot do, yet this is perhaps one of the most important things to learn about ministry. I can only do things effectively in God's strength and then only those tasks which he asks of me. The difficulty, however, is to determine what they are!

I was constantly struck by how busy clergy seem to be, and the variety of demands they have on their time. I felt very angry at the many bureaucratic and administrative demands there are upon clergy. Taking part on various committees made me aware of the load placed upon the vicar. I accept that so much of this is necessary, yet how frustrating for ministers who enter the ministry to serve God and their community and then find their hands full of bits of paper. Perhaps one day there will be fulltime administrators to allow clergy to concentrate on what they are called to do.

Coping with everyday living

I found switching off very difficult. My home began to feel like 'the office' and even when I was reading a book, writing letters, watching television, it was incredibly hard not to feel that there was something I could be doing, organizing, someone I could be ringing, visiting, etc. Then, just when I had been able to unwind, the phone would ring to remind me that the parish was still there! This was brought home to a greater degree when I lived in the vicarage. Nothing was sacred! I do not resent being 'available' to people, and accept that they are not always sensitive as to the time that they ring or call – this is all part of the sacrifice – but it does pose the question as to how you switch off and recharge, because I know through experience and observation that eventually you become totally ineffective, and I am sure that God does not intend this for his servants. I believe it is from him our strength comes, but also our rest! Jesus set an example of balance; however, in practice it is very difficult to achieve. I found that the only way really to relax was to get away physically, and I made a concerted effort to arrange things to take me out on a Saturday, or to entertain friends from outside the parish.

Something I feel I should mention at this point is the issue of being a single woman in ministry. It hardly needs saying that there persist in church life many traditional ideas and approaches towards women, some of which today are considered sexist. At times I found these difficult to handle and was often puzzled how to deal with them sensitively – a serious challenge to all women in ministry. I found certain attitudes especially hard having come from a working environment in which the majority of my colleagues were women and anti-sexist policies were burning issues. I was greatly helped by the parish deacon's presence, but in her absence I was painfully aware of how few women there are in ministry. Much of people's acceptance of me came from their knowledge of the deacon's excellent example. I feel that for a young single woman in ministry it is sometimes difficult for people to be able to identify with you – you can neither be placed in the traditional priestly role, nor that of the accepted norm for ministers, that of a family. I do not wish to say more about this as it is easy to allow such things to get out of perspective – we each have our individual cross to bear. I personally often perceived it to be a greater problem to others than to me.

Another issue which was of greater importance and concern to me during my placement was that of living alone with all the demands and stresses the job brings. How do you cope returning to an empty house from a particularly depressing visit or frustrating meeting? I found it very easy to get things out of perspective and difficult to allow adequate time for normal day to day things like coffee breaks and meals which are often good opportunities to share such things with someone. It is very easy to become introspective. On your own, who is going to tell you that you are perhaps reacting irrationally or working too hard? And who is there to actually force you to stop? Linked to this was the gulf of misunderstanding I found growing between myself and my friends who have little or no concept of what life for the ordained minister is like. I have since wondered whether it might have been helpful to have had an outside and independent person with whom I could have discussed various issues. This is not to negate nor detract from the time given to me by the vicar – however, sometimes a totally objective voice is helpful as well. Also it could have been helpful for the vicar to have had an outside resource for me to relate to when parish life became very hectic for him! I felt there were so many issues being raised and not the opportunity to talk them all through – one of the problems, I suppose, of living alone, for which solutions need to be found.

Attitudes to women in ministry and the problems of clergy living alone are issues which the Church needs to take an increasingly prayerful and considered look at.

The challenge of the parish
During my placement I found people's resistance to change on the sole grounds that 'It's the way we've always done things' difficult to understand. Inflexibility and intolerance I find very hard to comprehend as I feel increasingly that none of us has a monopoly of the truth. I frequently question why we cannot allow a variety of

styles of worship. However I really came to appreciate the pressure brought to bear on a minister by any kind of proposed change. Very often this kind of conflict results in ministers treading what must surely be a very lonely path. I realized how clergy silently 'suffer' for others, and how self-denying a true calling can be. Can you be humble enough to allow ideas and services to happen which you yourself would not choose to initiate and also defend the rights of individuals who cling to old patterns which you may equally disagree with? How do you listen to a variety of complaints with no one to appreciate your own? It is easier, of course, to gather like-minded souls and steer a single path, driving those who do not 'fit' to worship elsewhere, than to steer a way allowing something for all, but ensuring complaints as no one group will ever be satisfied. The danger, of course, is to drift too far the other way and try to satisfy everyone and lose sight of a vision of what God wants for his Church. It seems to me to be very important for ministers to maintain a personal vision to sustain them in times of disillusionment and despair.

The whole issue of change and of moving a church forward was one I was forced to consider. I feel my placement enabled me to experience at first hand the problems involved, and brought me to a real appreciation of the difficulties a minister is faced with in such situations. There appears to be a complex dilemma between complacency, consolidation, and challenge.

My placement church is a far more traditional setting than I am used to. However, even the most traditional structures I began to appreciate, if not necessarily agree with. My horizon and understanding were broadened considerably. Firstly my understanding of worship developed. Prior to my placement I felt that there were certain styles and ways of worshipping which were more 'correct' than others – however I came to appreciate that it's not so much the outward trappings, music, tradition, form of service, etc. which are important as the worshipful attitude of our hearts towards God. I feel that it is this attitude which most clearly communicates itself to others – when our worship is sincere and God-centred. I feel I appreciate more fully what worship is, and it is this which is the most crucial, yet most difficult, to communicate to a congregation. But I still feel that much of our worship needs to be more accessible and relevant to the society in which we live. I still have strong personal views on many issues, but these have become less important than encouraging others to find and develop their own personal faith, regardless of whether it matches how I would want it to be.

I even came to appreciate how many of the traditional groups were wonderful opportunities for exercising and developing ministry, and was delighted to find real faith in many unexpected areas. However, despite coming to a deeper appreciation of tradition, I continue to question how this speaks effectively to people today. I realize that this is something the Church shares with many ancient established

127

institutions, and that we are never to be dictated to by the ways of the world. I was increasingly led to wonder how we can witness and evangelize more effectively. I think there is more that we could be doing to actively witness for our faith today.

I especially grew to appreciate the opportunities of the traditional public services of the Church (baptism, marriages and funerals) to witness quietly and appropriately to others. This was quite a surprise to me as previously I had been quite disparaging of them.

My personal assessment of the placement

I feel in writing this 'report' it has been difficult for me to say how my expectations of ministry were changed, because as I began my placement I did not have any particular ideas as to what parish ministry was about. My main expectation was that I would learn a lot – and I did! What I have written is a reflection on what I experienced over the nine months.

I believe that my placement was invaluable. Previously I had a very limited understanding and partially informed idea of ministry. However, I had no conception of the diversity, complexity, and variety of parish life. My placement brought to the fore many important issues which needed, and will continue to need, prayerful consideration and working through. One of the most important aspects I found were the many challenges a different church tradition brought to my limited church experience, forcing me to rethink many of my firmly held beliefs. I was brought to quite a low point when I had to really consider what the Church stands for in our society, and the problems it faces in serving the community today. I found much of what I experienced very challenging and sometimes disturbing, but God really used the time to enable me to confront the many issues I will face in the future.

My placement has forewarned me of the stresses and pressures of the ordained life and has made me consider how I, in my own personal situation, need to find ways of coping. I am very grateful for the opportunities it has allowed me to experience different areas of ministry, showing me where further work and reflection are needed while at college.

I hope that the opportunity I have had is made increasingly available to others, perhaps even before the 'selection' stage, as there may be many people who have little or no idea of the life they are being called to. Taking the experience of the last nine months with me to theological college I have a constant touchstone to remind me of what my training is for – a reality check for all that I learn. I am able to ask how my three years at college relate to the experience I have had. I believe that I have had an invaluable opportunity to enter ministry with a far greater understanding of what it is all about, and a deeper appreciation of what God is *calling me to. Having been challenged and stretched during my placement I feel a greater openness to the opportunities and demands of college, with the spiritual, pastoral and theological challenges it offers for learning and reflection. Most important of all, it has made me far more open to other traditions and opinions. I thank God for all he has chosen to teach me through my placement, and it is my prayer that others may be so fortunate.*

The Society for Promoting Christian Knowledge (SPCK) was founded in 1698. Its mission statement is:

To promote Christian knowledge by

- **Communicating the Christian faith in its rich diversity**
- **Helping people to understand the Christian faith and to develop their personal faith; and**
- **Equipping Christians for mission and ministry**

SPCK Worldwide serves the Church through Christian literature and communication projects in 100 countries, and provides books for those training for ministry in many parts of the developing world. This worldwide service depends upon the generosity of others and all gifts are spent wholly on ministry programmes, without deductions.

SPCK Bookshops support the life of the Christian community by making available a full range of Christian literature and other resources, providing support for those training for ministry, and assisting bookstalls and book agents throughout the UK.

SPCK Publishing produces Christian books and resources, covering a wide range of inspirational, pastoral, practical and academic subjects. Authors are drawn from many different Christian traditions, and publications aim to meet the needs of a wide variety of readers in the UK and throughout the world.

The Society does not necessarily endorse the individual views contained in its publications, but hopes they stimulate readers to think about and further develop their Christian faith.

For information about the Society, visit our website at
www.spck.org.uk, or write to:
SPCK, Holy Trinity Church, Marylebone Road,
London NW1 4DU, United Kingdom.